PENTAGON PRESS

COMMITTED TO SERVE THE ARMED FORCES

AFGHANISTAN BEYOND 2014

Domestic and Regional Dynamics

AFGHANISTAN BEYOND 2014

Domestic and Regional Dynamics

Editor

Arpita Basu Roy

MAULANA ABUL KALAM AZAD INSTITUTE OF ASIAN STUDIES
KOLKATA

PENTAGON PRESS

Afghanistan Beyond 2014: Domestic and Regional Dynamics

Editor: Arpita Basu Roy

ISBN 978-81-8274-882-8

First Published in 2016

Published by
PENTAGON PRESS
206, Peacock Lane, Shahpur Jat,
New Delhi-110049
Phones: 011-64706243, 26491568
Telefax: 011-26490600
email: rajan@pentagonpress.in
website: www.pentagonpress.in

Branch
Flat No.213, Athena-2,
Clover Acropolis,
Viman Nagar,
Pune-411014
Email: pentagonpresspune@gmail.com

Printed at Avantika Printers Private Limited.

Contents

Contributors

Ahmad Fahim Hakim is a qualified social, development, and human rights advocate. Currently he is a human rights commissioner and deputy chair with the Afghanistan Independent Human Rights Commission (AIHRC).

Ajay Darshan Behera (Prof.) is Professor at the Academy of International Studies, Jamia Millia Islamia University, New Delhi. He is also the Coordinator of the Pakistan Studies Programme at the Academy.

Ambrish Dhaka (Dr.) is Associate Professor at School of International Studies, JNU, New Delhi. He specializes in Geopolitics and Ethno-political Studies.

Ahmadullah Archiwal is a PhD student, Rutgers University NJ, USA.

Alok Bansal is Director, India Foundation, New Delhi. He was also a Visiting Professor at Jamia Millia Islamia University and a Senior Fellow at the Centre for Land Warfare Studies (CLAWS), New Delhi.

Anwesha Ghosh is a doctoral candidate at the Willy Brandt School of Public Policy (University of Erfurt) under DAAD PhD Programme in International Conflict Management.

Bahram Amirahmadian (Prof.) is Visiting Professor, Faculty of World Studies, Tehran University, Tehran.

Chayanika Saxena is a President Scholar from South Asian University. She holds a Master's in International Relations, speaks Dari and is preparing for her Doctoral Research.

Elnara Bainazarova (Dr.) is a Postdoctoral researcher at "Proactive Conflict Management at Post-Soviet Deep Borders" project, Tampere Peace Research

Institute, Finland. She is Special Adviser on ODA-KazAID issues, Ministry of Foreign Affairs of the Republic of Kazakhstan.

Gulshan Sachdeva (Prof.) is Professor, School of International Studies, Jawaharlal Nehru University. Between 2006 and 2010 he headed the Asian Development Bank and The Asia Foundation projects on regional cooperation at the Afghanistan Ministry of Foreign Affairs in Kabul.

Ildar Yakubov (Dr.), is a PhD in Political Science and works with the Independent Institute for Monitoring the Formation of Civil Society, Uzbekistan.

Maqsudul Hasan Nuri (Dr.) is Adviser, International Relations (Department of Humanities), COMSATS Institute of Information and Technology, Islamabad, Pakistan.

Rana Banerji is Distinguished Fellow at the Institute for Peace & Conflict Studies, New Delhi and Visiting Professor, Pakistan Studies Programme at the Academy of International Relations, Jamia Millia Islamia University, Delhi. He is former Special Secretary, Cabinet Secretariat, GOI.

Saurabh Kumar is pursuing BA LLB from WBNUJS, Kolkata and a former research intern at MAKAIAS.

Tariq Rather is Associate Professor and the Coordinator of conferences at the Centre of Central Asian Studies, University of Kashmir, Hazratbal Srinagar, Jammu and Kashmir, India.

Wadir Safi is Professor, Law and Political Science, Kabul University and Vice-President, Afghanistan Justice Organization, Kabul. He served as Dean of the Law and Political Science Faculty of Kabul University for six years in the eighties.

Y. Emre Gurbuz is Associate Professor, Department of History, Kyrgyz-Turkish Manas University. He is the Vice-Dean of Faculty of Letters and Vice-Chairman of Turkic Civilization Research and Application Center.

Introduction

Afghanistan faces an arduous transition subject to myriad variables. Fluidity and flux has remained constant in Afghanistan's political history and stays mirrored in its contemporary reality as uncertainties of an international troop withdrawal and apprehensions of internal power struggle loom large. Located at the interface of three distinct regions—Central Asia, West Asia and South Asia, traditionally, the country has served as a buffer state for major powers and its current borders which were drawn in the late 19th century with the declared aim of preventing conflict, arguably, still remains the site of proxy wars or political competition for other states. Fixated on Afghanistan's looming challenges, often a bleak picture of the embattled country's future is being drawn in the international media and academia which anticipate that the volatility of Afghanistan would lead to regional instability and colossal security challenges, especially in the period beyond 2014. And that regional order which is yet to emerge is a pressing need in order to avoid intensified regional rivalry. However, the narrative of despair is supplemented by a narrative of opportunity where proposals envisioning Afghanistan's role as a fulcrum for trade and cooperation are being drawn up on the basis of an argument that hegemonic prescriptions do not sustain themselves. Nation-building, it is said, could proceed on the basis of economic development, social harmony, rule of law and participatory democracy in consonance with the "wishes of the Afghan people".

Contemporary Afghanistan remains a complex milieu characterised by powerful and competing agendas. Variables like the Taliban insurgency, the capabilities of the Afghan National Security Forces, presence of international troops, the internal power struggle and the regional dynamics are fast evolving and altering. India, an active player in Afghanistan has legitimate concerns about the kind of role it is to play under such circumstances. The post-2014 situation and the possibility of an international withdrawal necessitates, sharing concerns, evaluating the contingencies and preparing beyond. The aim of this volume is to provide a dispassionate assessment of the country's future on the following themes: internal political dynamics and power-struggle in Afghanistan, criticalities of security transition in Afghanistan, reconciliation between the other ethnic groups and the Taliban, possibilities of an "Afghan-owned" and "Afghan-led" process, regional security and the role of the regional countries, global response to the Afghan issue, India's and Pakistan's security dilemma vis-a-vis Afghanistan and India's workable response.

Afghanistan: Domestic Dynamics

The fall of the Taliban regime in 2001 heralded more than a decade of international efforts to rebuild the country and re-establish political order. This effort, while achieving some major successes, remains incomplete. It is frustrated from the outside by a resilient insurgency and undermined from within by government structures criticized as corrupt and often predatory. The international presence now is declining significantly, opening into a "transition decade" marked by Afghans presumably in a position to take greater responsibility for their own security and economic development.

Assuming responsibility for an economy that has been almost exclusively dependent on outside assistance for more than a decade Afghanistan post 2014 indeed faces an arduous economic transition. Gulshan Sachdeva in his paper *Economic Challenges in Post-2014 Afghanistan* is however optimistic that economic recovery and removal of corruption will be attempted by the new national unity government. He feels so because at the Bonn as well as Tokyo conferences, both the international community as well as the regional players re-affirmed their long-term commitment to the future of Afghanistan, which goes much beyond 2014. There have also been discussions on working for a *New Silk Road Strategy* for Afghanistan. Despite optimism, he is sceptic on several other counts as he feels that these developments fail to reduce uncertainty about Afghanistan's future. He apprehends that with the declining western interest, the amount of resources available for development projects is likely to be significantly lower than the past one decade. He argues that withdrawals of international troops in other parts of the world have reduced civilian aid, with implications for economic growth and fiscal sustainability. Therefore, potential financing gaps in the budget could threaten security and recent progress made at the developmental front. He also argues that within the broad context of increasing regional economic cooperation, India would continue to support both the Regional Economic Cooperation Conference on Afghanistan (RECCA) as well as and the "Heart of Asia" processes.

Reconciliation is a viable solution to the political and security related problems in Afghanistan. However, most regional players need to support an 'Afghan-led and Afghan-owned' peace and reconciliation process while internal actors in Afghanistan need to resolve the issue politically through peaceful means. Ahmad Fahim Hakim in his paper on the *Prospects of an "Afghan-owned" and "Afghan-led" process for national reconciliation* has specifically pointed out that the notion of 'Afghan-led and Afghan-owned' peace process would only work, when efforts at the national, regional and international levels are well coordinated. At the national level the Afghan government needs to effectively strengthen 'good governance' and promote constitutional political order, demonstrate strong political will in curbing corruption and supporting meritocracy in all official appointments, and to ensure people's access to justice, while putting an end to impunity. At the regional level, the regional countries are willing to revisit their narratives for regional peace and stability and to work towards addressing the root causes of extremism in the region; and to enhance economic and commercial cooperation at the regional level through existing regional mechanisms. And at the international level, the international community should maintain its long-term commitment and support effective 'nation-building' and 'state-building' process in Afghanistan and enhance its efforts to promote democracy and human rights in the region, and the timely engagement of the UN to play its mediatory task to complement the so called 'Afghan-led and Afghan-owned' peace process.

In complex post-conflict environments, such as Afghanistan, security and development needs are intertwined. Without addressing both at the same time, it would be hard to ensure an enabling environment for sustainable economic growth or political reconciliation. Wadir Safi in his paper *Security and*

Development in Afghanistan after 2014 argues that the increase of instability and insecurity are not the only threats to Afghanistan after 2014. He fears that all that has been achieved in the past decade might be threatened as the region will be more unsafe after the withdrawal as violence is likely to increase. Mass exodus of civilians due to the fear of conflict may throw up massive challenges for the international organizations and other countries. He feels that the lack of assistance to maintain the operations will cause loss of control at the central levels; disable the operations and presence of national army and national police forces leading to human rights violations, increase of insurgent attacks and interventions of vested interest groups. He believes that Afghanistan still needs support of international community. UN and the international community should continue their efforts for peace building and development. The role of UN should be enhanced and their strategies for development and security need to be improved.

Afghanistan has a legacy of 35 years of conflict and one of the world's largest populations in protracted displacement with the year 2014 marking another watershed in this legacy. The country 'in transition' is in considerable uncertainty about its capacity to address the challenges of repatriation, integration and reintegration and continuing displacement. Anwesha Ghosh in her paper *Afghan Migration 2014 and Beyond: A Regional Perspective* argues that years of war, conflict and human rights abuse profoundly shook Afghanistan and pushed a third of its population to exile. Afghan refugees long constituted the world's largest refugee population and one of the most protracted situations in the world. They have also been subject of the largest repatriation undertaken since 2002—a process that is still ongoing. The paper provides a brief overview of the major phases of population movement out of Afghanistan before focusing at final phase (2002-2014), which interestingly witnessed movements, both in and out of Afghanistan. The year 2014 marked a watershed for Afghanistan and the regional countries which host substantial Afghan refugee population. Series of assumptions and rough calculations were undertaken to deal with the situation flowing from the inevitable drawdown of financial and technical assistance and the formidable challenges those developments might pose. A cursory glance at the recent migration trend confirm that the need of assistance for displaced people are increasing at a time when the international and regional commitment to support humanitarian activities in Afghanistan are decreasing. Under these circumstances, she espouses a holistic perspective on the unfolding migration scene and its impact for Afghanistan and the region.

A 'democratisation' process, marked by elections, with limited attempts at institution building, has continued since 2001, with varying degrees of success. While the successful entrenchment of democratic principles necessitates a sense of national unity and economic development, critics have maintained that Afghanistan, which has, for most of its history, been economically poor, ravaged by war and is characterised by a highly decentralised tribal societal structure unsuited to Western model of democracy, installing a strong government at the centre through the mechanism of elections was an ambitious project. Chayanika Saxena in her paper *Democratic Transition in Afghanistan and Popular Reflections,* however, enunciates that having experimented with the idea of 'democratic' governance in the past, this model of political ordering is certainly not new to Afghanistan. However, what is new are the attempts that are being made to sustain this semblance of order in a country that has been affected by decades of in-fighting and the colossal damages that have been caused on its account. As this latest entrant into South Asia took its turn towards democracy, riding on both the international support and domestic participation, Afghanistan could succeed in transiting from a political regime of extreme repression (Taliban) to democracy, and subsequently, in passing the reins to the successors within this order. Despite being mired in charges of corruption and inefficacy, the transitions—both to and within the democratic order—is notable. However, there still remains a yawning gap between the popular and international expectations and reality. The Taliban that is on the rise again; the central government machinery that has not been able to penetrate into the different corners of Afghanistan; the rescinding international interest and a flailing economy have all begun contributing to the dwindling faith of the masses in the government, and thereby the democratic order within which it is working. While all hope is not lost in Afghanistan, the above mentioned developments have surely shaken the faith of international spectators and domestic constituencies in the political trajectory that is being followed. As such, this paper provides an estimate of the developments that have taken place on the turf of democracy in Afghanistan since 2001, with reflections from the Afghan diaspora in Kolkata (*Kabuliwalas*) providing an expatriates' account of it. Steering through the major feats and the setbacks democracy encountered (and continues to), this paper attempts at assessing how democracy has unfolded in this country, and how it is has been viewed by the Afghans within and outside the borders of their country. The scope of the paper is to provide voice to the common, popular expressions on a question so important: how has democracy fared in Afghanistan?

Afghanistan and the Region

Afghanistan has always occupied a position of geopolitical significance and has been the meeting place of ecological and cultural areas although it is landlocked and seemingly isolated. West Asia, Central Asia, the Indian subcontinent, and even the Far East have influenced this territory and vice versa. Shared identities and networks span borders and facilitate human activities over which the state has little or no control. Yet, the security concerns upheld by individual states, as they situate themselves within their respective regions, remain essential. And, while many of the states in the larger neighbourhood are weak in many respects, they tend to command significant coercive capacity. Traditional conceptions of security, in which protecting vital state interests is the primary aim and military power is the key instrument, remain dominant. Although each neighbouring country has generally tried to stay out of the turmoil within Afghanistan, in many cases neighbouring states have felt obligated to support or assist one side or another in order to protect their own internal stability.

Afghanistan's recent history clearly demonstrates that the regional context and external involvement can make or break a peacebuilding process. Afghanistan is situated in a region marked by a range of conflicts, and the interests of different state and non-state actors often run counter to the peace building process in the country. It is being argued in academic and policy circles that it is in particular interest of regional states to stabilize the volatility within the area and develop a joint approach towards Afghanistan that can secure a more lasting peace. It is more or less accepted that it is not possible to resolve the challenges internal to Afghanistan without addressing the security challenges of its neighbours. Therefore it has often been reiterated that a regional approach and a regional strategy is required that includes Pakistan, India, the Central Asian States and even China and Russia along with perhaps at some point Iran.

Much ink has been spilled over Pakistan's troubled relations with India than about Islamabad's difficult relationship with its neighbour to the west. Historically, the chief driver of Afghanistan-Pakistan tensions has been their disputed border, the 1,500-mile Durand Line and tensions continue to mar the relation even today with hopes of a negotiated settlement in the ongoing 13-year war look very bleak. Ajay D Behera in *Pakistan's Dilemmas in the Afghan Endgame* argues that it is still difficult to comprehend how the endgame is likely to play out. Negotiations with the Taliban are unlikely to succeed and there are many other imponderables and the most important being how Pakistan views the endgame and what role it can play in the endgame. Whether the Taliban weakens or strengthens has largely to do with Pakistan. It continues to be functional because of the sanctuaries in Pakistan and in support of the Pakistan army. It is not clear whether Islamabad is serious about promoting stability in Afghanistan or is merely making token moves to deflect Western criticism of Pakistan's record in Afghanistan. Stability in Afghanistan is critical to Pakistan's security and development. Pakistan needs to be worried about the potential destabilization of Afghanistan that could follow the US-NATO withdrawal. Possible results could include millions of new refugees if a civil war breaks out in Afghanistan and the scary prospect for Pakistan of reverse sanctuary for the TTP and other anti-state actors. Therefore, the continuing support for the Taliban despite the pressures suggests skewed national priorities. He points out that it is not clear to what extent Pakistan's strategic elites think that their muddled policy of supporting the Taliban has gravely compromised their security.

On the other hand, several analysts and policy makers have pointed out that Pakistan and Afghanistan have a unique opportunity to turn around the negative developments into a gainful opportunity. Maqsudul Hasan Nuri in his paper on *Pakistan's Angst in Post-2014 Scenario* indicates that the transition in Afghanistan is going to be tumultuous at least for the first five years or so—depending upon a host of factors: domestic, regional and global. He argues that despite attempts at democratisation, Afghan politics remain predominantly feudalistic and tribal, where questions of honour, revenge and bloodshed dominate views of leadership at all levels. Besides, he is critical towards Afghanistan when he points out that Afghanistan has developed a "rentier mentality" in history to play one rival against the other for financial rewards. It still lacks adequate infrastructure of roads and railways, judicial system and industry. In this backdrop the primary questions of his paper is to analyse some of the major concerns of Pakistan after US/NATO military withdrawal by end of 2014. These concerns include the fresh influx of refugees in case of fresh crises involving Afghanistan, use of drone technology and the Indian role in Afghanistan. He however feels that both countries have a unique opportunity to mend the fences and engage in cooperative projects towards which the international community should contribute. Many opine that normalization and eventual settlement of Kashmir dispute between India and Pakistan could help unlock doors for cooperation in Afghanistan too. He hopes that this may bring about an opportunity whereby the underperforming SAARC region could open up greater economic activity after the post-2014 US transition.

Iran has close linguistic and cultural ties to Afghanistan, particularly with Tajiks, Persian-speaking Afghans in Herat Province, and the Hazara, a Shiite minority residing in central and northern Afghanistan and has legitimate concerns regarding the situation in Afghanistan. Iranian influence in this region runs deep and Iran may play a positive role in stabilizing its war-ravaged neighbour. *Bahram Amirahmadian* in his paper on *The Iranian Government and Afghanistan* questions the effectiveness of the presence of coalition forces as there is continuation of instability and terrorism. He enquires as to why the situation has not changed in the desired direction? One of the key elements of the continuation of *Talibanism* is that it is supported by domestic residents of rural areas and financed by outside actors and the tribal structure of the societies of the border areas, cannot be controlled by the governments of two sides. He enunciates the problems that Iran faces as a result of continuing conflict in Afghanistan, one of which is the inflow of Afghans into Iran which puts pressure on its economy and deprives Iranian of jobs that Afghans take up. Illegal marriages, he says impacts Iranian society as Iranian women marries Afghan men. For preserving Iranian borders against Afghan smugglers and drugs trafficking, Iran needs a huge budget to employ a lot of military forces and equipment in the borders. On the other hand he feels that Iran likes to have a very close multilateral cooperation with Afghanistan in several fields. Iran considers Afghanistan as a friend and brother country with many common strands in culture and history, with common Persian language and would like to share its development in industry, agriculture and cultural issue with Afghanistan. When Afghanistan becomes stable, he hopes, it is natural that Afghan refugees from Iran will be able to return to their own country and this change will improve the economic, cultural and social situation in Iran. Iran is interested to improve the economic situation in Afghanistan and in the fields of education, agricultural sector to replace economic corps instead of opium production. He discusses at some length about the details of the possibilities of economic cooperation between Iran and Afghanistan.

Central Asia has numerous important ties to Afghanistan- historical, cultural, geographic and demographic. Central Asia may not see an immediate explosion of violence and militancy after the U.S. and NATO drawdown from Afghanistan in 2014. However, Central Asia's internal issues and the region's many links with Afghanistan—including a web of relationships among militant groups—will add to the volatility in the region. *Elnara Bainazarova* in her paper *Soft Power Diplomacy of Kazakhstan—New Approach Towards Regional Security?* argues that the post-2014 situation prompts Central Asian states to pursue new foreign policy approaches to address the emerging security challenges. She argues that security in Central Asia is challenged by several factors of national development in Afghanistan, which still lacks public institutions and is burdened with a weak economy. She reasons that regional politics is creating a new security environment for the dynamically developing Kazakhstan, which is striving to implement new soft power tools in the region, relying on the principles of Asian regionalism. In her paper she shows how Kazakhstan is interested in sustainable and stable development of Afghanistan and is ready to work with international partners to promote the socio-economic rehabilitation of the country. The reforms in foreign policy concept of Kazakhstan is striving to implement multilateralism, non-formality, consensus—and has features of Asian regionalism with a special emphasis on official development assistance program (ODA) for Central Asia and Afghanistan and a special operating agency.

The volume also focuses on two other Central Asian states—Uzbekistan and Kyrgyzstan and their threat perceptions vis-a-vis Afghanistan. *Ildar Yakubov* in his paper on *Afghan Factor in the Regional Security of Central Asia* states that regional security threats in Central Asia, emanating from Afghanistan is felt most clearly in neighboring countries and Uzbekistan is severely affected among them. Its position and relations with Afghanistan play an important role in ensuring regional security and in stabilizing the situation within Afghanistan. This he feels would be an important contribution to the peace process. Implementation of reconstruction projects will help in stabilizing the situation in Afghanistan. Such efforts appear to be the most promising in the current context of the Islamic Republic of Afghanistan. Uzbekistan has to actualize the need for rapid response to security threats and challenges emanating from Afghanistan. It gives the opportunity to minimize the inevitable damage of the growing tensions in regional security, and improve resilience to external risks. *Y. Emre Gürbüz*'s paper on *Afghanistan after the US Withdrawal: A Look from Kyrgyzstan* argues that the withdrawal of the US troops necessitates wider, deeper, more constructive and lasting alliances and also favours Afghan-led solutions to the complex situation in Afghanistan. He believes that after the withdrawal, regional powers are expected to take on a more active role in Afghanistan. A shift might may occur replacing the US-led ISAF operation to an Afghan-led operation with the support of regional states. His articles begins by detailing the key air base of the US troops operating in Afghanistan i.e. the Manas Air base. It also focuses on the implications of the US withdrawal from Central Asia with a view from Kyrgyzstan.

India and Afghanistan

Political developments, economic changes and social transformation within Afghanistan remain vital for India. Afghanistan's fate cannot be disentangled from that of the region and in the same light one can argue that a stable Afghanistan relates to India's immediate foreign policy objectives of a peaceful periphery, good relations with neighbours, transformation of relations with the major powers and cooperation with the international community on a host of issues. Bilateral relations between the Republic of India and the Islamic State of Afghanistan have been traditionally strong and friendly. India considers Afghanistan to be its neighbour as the Gilgit-Baltistan region of Kashmir which borders Wakhan, although under Pakistani control, is claimed by India as a border between the nations. India's engagement in the country remains crucial more because there is a gradual acceptability by the international community for a role that India can play as a provider of regional stability.

However India's engagement with Afghanistan has been an unswerving source of concern for the common neighbour, Pakistan. Pakistan is deeply suspicious of Indian influence across its western border. For much of its history, Pakistan has pursued a policy of "strategic depth" in Afghanistan by training, funding, and arming groups that can act as proxies for Pakistani interests. Pakistan is concerned that India's economic and political linkages are building up Indian capacity to destabilize Pakistan. It definitely sees both India and Afghanistan as relevant to its own national security and, accordingly, responds to actual and perceived threats in its relations with both states. Pakistan, like many postcolonial states, has time and again faced the threat of internal fragmentation and has accused India and Afghanistan of supporting separatist movements within its territory. Therefore, India's engagement in Afghanistan is considered to be a security threat by Pakistan. Post-2014 dynamics within Afghanistan and that in the region will have direct impact on India and the trilateral dynamics between India, Pakistan and Afghanistan will likely to play it out after the withdrawal of international forces.

India's policy vis-a-vis Afghanistan, therefore, need to be carefully calibrated to suit the interest of both countries and that India should be careful enough not to undo the goodwill that it has earned over the years through reconstruction activities. Ambrish Dhaka and Ahmadullah Archiwal in their paper *India's Afghanistan Policy post-2014 in need of Geopolitical Constructivism* argue that a comprehensive policy for India would be one where India's Afghanistan policy carries the Indian intent in the region. And India need to give a preferential ordering of the issues which India would like to promote in Afghanistan and denounce those which India thinks can be harmful regionally. They suggest that India need to strengthen parliamentary democracy, have multi-lateral investment policy, promote UN and SCO mandate for ANSF training, support ethno-political pluralism, Afghan-led and owned process, support the constitutional and legal framework of the State. There are certain suggestion for various situational responses in the wake of the ebb and flow of Afghanistan's political stability. They argue that there is fair degree of indication that for India to have a successful Afghanistan policy it has to take into confidence all those Pashtun-led political groups who stand for political pluralism and are averse to any monopolising force (including Taliban) bent upon capturing the Afghan state.

The way things shape out will have a direct impact on India's security. It is therefore in India's interests to ensure that the events in Afghanistan shape up in a manner that they do not threaten India's long term security and interests. Alok Bansal in his paper *Afghanistan post 2014: Implications for India and Indian Options* argues that Pakistan is trying to convince the Western world that a lasting peace in Afghanistan is unlikely without co-opting Taliban. A weary American administration, which desperately needs a face saver, is buying the Pakistani argument. Numerous attempts are being made to negotiate with the Taliban, which are in no way contributing towards peace. The future of Afghanistan to a great extent thereafter will depend on the security guarantees and financial support that the country receives from international community. Any presence of an obscurantist radical outfit like Taliban within the power structures in Kabul, threatens India's security and it is therefore essential that India must have a proactive policy to ensure that an independent and strong Afghanistan capable of keeping Taliban at bay, emerges after withdrawal of the troops from United States and its allies. He suggests that India needs to set up training facilities in Afghanistan with Indian training teams for imparting necessary skills to the personnel from ANA. India needs to understand that failure in Afghanistan is not an option and Taliban in Kabul is akin to Taliban at Wagha and poses an extremely grave threat to India's existence as a thriving secular democracy

Afghanistan beyond 2014 apprehends many uncertainties which would require India not to become complacent yet remain ready with flexible and balanced responses. Rana Banerji in his paper *India's Security and Strategic Concerns vis-a-vis Pakistan's role* has enunciated that Pakistani consideration is to limit India's role and presence in Afghanistan, at best to development activities sans any political clout on the power brokers who emerge in Kabul.

And he also presupposes that Pakistan could retaliate against India with political, economic, and military pressure by taking certain steps. In his paper Banerji proposes that India should remain prepared to continue its diplomatic and developmental engagement in Afghanistan, with whosoever comes to power there, depending also on the nature of relationship and requests for assistance that are received from the new government in Kabul. He proposes that as back up option, India could consider reviving old friendships in uncertain power equilibrium and even think of cultivating new Pashtun friends, if these are of moderate hue and eschew radical links.

However it is understandable that any way forward in the relationships must take into account not only internal stability in Afghanistan but greater stability in India–Pakistan relations which has a direct bearing on Kashmir. *Tareak A. Rather* in his paper on the *Impact of Afghan Drawdown on Kashmir* is apprehensive about the diplomatic war of two neighbours, India and Pakistan, on Kashmir which may unfold in Afghanistan in the near future. He argues that the Afghan situation is quite fragile and vulnerable to all sorts of influences and this fighting could easily turn into a regional proxy war and it is very essential to begin a meaningful dialogue on Kashmir. All this can be done by taking three purposeful initiatives and factoring them in any future policy instrument on Afghanistan. The three initiatives could be categorised into: improving the internal situation within Pakistan, resumption of India-Pakistan dialogue process, consolidation of gains and mapping the future course of action in Kashmir. How India will respond to the whole twists and turns of Pakistan's diplomacy regarding Kashmir and Afghanistan remains to be seen.

There are regional and international responses to the Indian engagement. Similarly there are shortcomings of the engagement which need to be factored into the post 2014 dynamics. Saurabh Kumar in his paper *Indian Engagement in Afghanistan (Post 2001): A Critical Analysis* argues that Indian involvement in Afghanistan can be viewed to be an instance of using calculated soft power to help a war-torn nation recover. His paper tries to answer certain questions: How India got involved? How has India tried helping Afghanistan and how successful has this been? How has the international community responded to Indian aid, specifically Pakistan and the western nations engaged in

Afghanistan who can frame Afghanistan's future? What have been the shortcomings of India's Afghan engagement and the challenges that India face? And most importantly, what does the future hold for Indo-Afghan relationship and Indian involvement in rebuilding the strife torn country? He contends that while NATO-led forces strive for a military victory over Taliban-led insurgency movement, Indian help, primarily aimed at Afghan masses, aims at winning hearts to win this war.

Afghanistan: Domestic Dynamics

1

Economic Challenges in Post-2014 Afghanistan

Gulshan Sachdeva

With a new national unity government in place and Bilateral Security Agreement (BSA) with the US signed and ratified, things are getting clearer in Afghanistan. Irrespective of what happens with the Afghan peace process, it is clear that a new phase of Afghanistan project is going to begin from 2015. Apart from focusing security, the new government has also indicated that it would prioritize economic recovery and removing corruption.

Earlier, most analysts and international reports had indicated that in the post-2014 phase, the country is going to face three major challenges – security, political and economic. The economic challenge is by no means less serious than security and political difficulties. At the Bonn, Istanbul and Tokyo conferences, both the international community as well as the regional players re-affirmed their long-term commitment to the future of Afghanistan, which goes much beyond 2014. There are also discussions on working for a New Silk Road Strategy for Afghanistan.

These developments, however, fail to reduce uncertainty about Afghanistan's future. It is becoming clear that with declining western interest, the amount of resources available for development projects in the next decade is likely to be significantly lower than the past one decade. Experience suggests that withdrawals of international troops in other parts of the world have reduced civilian aid, with implications for economic growth and fiscal sustainability. Therefore, potential financing gaps in the budget could threaten security and recent progress made at the developmental front. According to the World Bank, actual aid to Afghanistan in 2010-11 was about $16 billion, about the size of the nominal GDP. Any rapid decline in aid will severely affect growth performance and employment scenario in the country. According to the *Asian Development Bank*, the planned foreign troop pullout by 2014 may lower growth by at least 2-3 percentage points. Despite international commitment for the "transformation decade of 2005-2014", Afghan government will be forced to deploy its limited resources on maintaining security infrastructure.

To offset these trends, Afghanistan has to concentrate on two things. First, it has to attract foreign investment particularly in sectors like mining, hydrocarbons, infrastructure, telecommunications, agriculture, education, health services etc. Secondly, for long term sustainability, it ultimately also has to play its traditional role of facilitating trade and commerce through its territories. In both these areas, regional countries could play a very significant role. Both the Delhi Investment Summit on Afghanistan, organised by Confederation of Indian Industry (CII) in 2012 as well as Doing Business with Afghanistan meeting organised by Federation of Indian Chambers of Commerce & Industry (FICCI) in 2013 emphasized precisely on these two points. The choice of India for these investment summits was also important as many Indian companies have already decided on big investments in Afghanistan. A consortium of seven Indian companies led by the state-owned Steel Authority of India (SAIL) have won a $10.3bn deal to mine three iron ore blocks in central Afghanistan. Some Indian companies are also planning to bid for copper and gold projects. There are also reports that India is also planning to build a 900 Km railway line between Iran's Chabahar port and Bamiyan province where Indian companies are planning large investments. India has also allocated $ 100 million for upgradation of Chabahar port in Iran to improve its trade with Afghanistan and Central Asia.

Strategic location of Afghanistan will always be important for India, particularly in the context of difficult India-Pakistan relations. However, importance of Afghanistan for India is much bigger than normally perceived in this narrow context. Once Afghanistan becomes stable, trade through Pakistan and Afghanistan could also alter India's continental trade. Within a few years, India's trade with Europe, CIS plus Iran, Afghanistan and Pakistan would be about US$ 400-500 billion annually. Even if 20 per cent of this trade is conducted through road, US$ 100-120 billion of Indian trade would be passing through Afghanistan and Central Asia. With improvement in India-Pakistan relations, an important portion of Indian trade (particularly from the landlocked northern states including Jammu & Kashmir) will be moving through Pakistan and Afghanistan. With the possibility of this trade passing through Afghanistan and Central Asia, most of the infrastructural projects in the region will become economically viable. These linkages will also transform small and medium industries and agriculture in Central Asia and Afghanistan. A major impediment in realising this potential is existing difficult relations between India and Pakistan. While looking at the regional economic dynamics, it is clear that both India and Pakistan would be paying huge economic costs for not cooperating in the Afghanistan. If trade stops in Pakistan, many road and other infrastructural projects will never become viable because of low volumes. Direct linkages between Central Asia and India will also give huge boost to all economies in the region, particularly to Afghanistan.

For many of these things to happen, various big and small projects discussed at different meetings in the last few years need clear prioritisation. A few studies have indicated immediate and long term measures which can soften the economic impact of military drawdown and create conditions for self sustained growth. Earlier, it was thought that Afghanistan has very limited resources. The Afghanistan government in 2010 claimed, however, that the country has huge untapped mineral resources worth at least 3 trillion dollars. Afghan and American officials have now repeatedly talked about the New Silk Road Strategy. Since 2005, the idea has been discussed at many academic and policy forums. This strategy is a long term vision of an international trade, transit and energy network that links Central and South Asian economies through Afghanistan. This was a good blueprint for Afghanistan but unfortunately has been mixed with regional geopolitics and exit strategies from Afghanistan. Still, Afghanistan has no other option but to continuously working for this strategy.

This is true that it is difficult to imagine implementation of this policy in the present tensed political environment in the region. However, some positive developments have taken place. The Afghan-Pakistan Transit Trade Agreement (APTTA) has been reached after years of negotiations and active US encouragement. Under the agreement, both Afghanistan and Pakistan have agreed to facilitate the movement of goods between and through their respective territories. Pakistan has allowed Afghan exports to India through Wagah and to China through Sost/Tashkurgan. Similarly, Afghanistan has allowed Pakistani trucks to reach Tajikistan, Turkmenistan, Uzbekistan and Iran through its territories. Afghan trucks can carry Afghan transit export cargo on designated routes up to Pakistani sea ports of Karachi, Qasim, Gwadar and Wagah border. At the moment, this is only a partial agreement as Afghan cargo is offloaded on to Indian trucks back to back at Wagah and trucks on return are not allowed to carry Indian exports back to Afghanistan. Despite its limited nature and serious initial problems in implementation, the agreement can be seen as a major development in regional economic cooperation. It has also generated interest beyond Afghanistan and Pakistan. Both Pakistan and Afghanistan have decided, in principle, to include Tajikistan also into APTTA. To make this initial small project into a serious regional economic force, it is imperative to include Turkmenistan, Uzbekistan (and perhaps Iran) into the broader agreement. However, the project will be of very limited interest to Central Asian countries if traffic to India is not allowed in both the directions. Once Central Asians and India are included in the expanded APTTA, the region will be ready to take advantage from the emerging Eurasian Economic Union space within a few years. Therefore, India needs to raise issue of APPTA implementation and its extension to India at every international forum.

Despite tensions at the political level, there are some positive developments between India and Pakistan on trade matters. Both have agreed on three agreements viz., redressal of trade grievances, mutual recognition and custom cooperation. Pakistan will allow bilateral trade through Wagah for all goods (presently restricted to 137 items). India has agreed to reduce number of items under restricted list by 30 per cent. There are some signs that Pakistan may provide MFN status to India soon. While India had given Pakistan MFN in 1996, Pakistan has been refusing to do so. Once that happens, India will bring SAFTA sensitive list to just 100. Pakistan will do so in the next five years. By 2020 peak tariff rate will not be more than 5 per cent. Both have also agreed to cooperate in investment, banking, electricity and gas trade, railways and better air connectivity. In addition, they have signed new liberalised visa regime.

In the last few years, all four countries involved in the TAPI project have already signed most agreements required for its commencement. These include: an Inter-Governmental Agreement (IGA), a Gas Pipeline Framework Agreement (GPFA) and Gas Sales and Purchase agreement. A broad agreement on transit fee has also been agreed upon. In November 2014, all four participating countries established TAPI Ltd and decided to start work on the project by 2015. The Indian public sector giant ONGC also plans to bring Russian hydrocarbons to India via Central Asia, Afghanistan and Pakistan. If implemented, these projects could become a 'game changer' in regional geo-politics and regional economic integration. They also have the potential to smoothen the 'Decade of Transformation' for Afghanistan.

Within the broad context of increasing regional economic cooperation, India continue to support both the Regional Economic Cooperation Conference on Afghanistan (RECCA) as well as and the "Heart of Asia" processes. In the Istanbul process India leads TCI-CBM. Uncertainty concerning post-2014 Afghanistan has also added new dimension to India's relations to Central Asian republics. The failure of Afghanistan project poses common security challenges but any positive outcome will open tremendous economic opportunities to both India and Central Asia. These two factors have increased strategic significance of the region considerably and are perhaps reasons for announcing a twelve point new 'Connect Central Asia' policy. Apart from other things the new policy initiative emphasizes on stepping up multilateral engagement (SCO, Eurasian Economic Union); reactivating International North South Trade Corridor and; strengthening strategic and security cooperation (military training, joint research, counterterrorism cooperation, close consultations on Afghanistan). As SCO may play a bigger role in Afghanistan in any post-2014 situation, India is also hoping to get its full membership soon.

Overall, all these developments indicate that compared to other western nations which are planning to reduce their engagement after 2014, India and other countries in the region are preparing for an enhanced engagement in the country. Reasons for enhanced engagement may vary from country to country. Enhanced Indian role is based on the assessment that international support to Afghanistan will continue much beyond 2014 and there is little scope for any 'negotiated settlement' in the near future.

2

Prospects of an "Afghan-owned" and "Afghan-led" process for national reconciliation

Ahmad Fahim Hakim

Afghanistan since 2001, after the disappearance of Taliban regime, has gone through a new political environment, which increased people's hope for a peaceful and prosperous future. They experienced two presidential, two parliamentary, and two provincial council elections since then. However, after almost thirteen years of international community's engagement (political and military support) and positive development on social and political arenas, Afghan women and men have mixed feelings about their future.

In 2014, Afghanistan would experience withdrawal of international forces, military and political transition and enhance a new process for transformation. Despite creating an opportunity for Afghans, 2014 would pose many challenges as well, in particular regarding political settlement and negotiation with Taliban.

Many research outcomes, conducted by national and international institutions recently, have highlighted that security is perceived as a top priority and main concern by all Afghans for a democratic, inclusive, and legitimate election in 2014.

The continuation of fighting and violence in the last decade has shown that there would be no military solution (preferably like Sri Lanka) for the current dilemma in Afghanistan for neither side: the Afghan government, NATO and ISAF, and the Taliban and other armed groups. The idea for a political settlement and reconciliation with Taliban and other warring factions fighting the Afghan Government has, therefore, been gaining ground in the last couple of years.

What possible scenarios we would foresee for future of Afghanistan:

1. A Peaceful Afghanistan: Where there is no more fighting. The international forces would leave the country, the Afghan National Security Forces (ANSF) are fully in charge of security, and the 2014 upcoming election is taking place producing a new leadership for the country, acceptable to all, where Taliban and Hezb-e-Islami (Hekmatyar) are merged to the constitutional political order[1]. They are part of the new government and would continue political competitions rather than military confrontation. Opportunities for a wide range of development and economic activities are increasing, and a peaceful and stable future is on the horizon. This, however, is an ideal situation, but not the most likely scenario to happen!

2. Status quo: Fighting continues (road side bombs, suicide attacks, civilian casualties, emergency and rehabilitation activities no long-term development schemes, NATO and ISAF forces would shuttle between combat and supportive roles to ANSF (military deadlock), elections would face challenges (insecurity, frauds, however with an accepted outcome[2]), weak government (though with new coalition with Hezb-e-Islami) would struggle to improve security and remain busy with minor reforms, while Taliban (new generation of Taliban) would continue to their violent confrontation and fight. This scenario is somehow likely to happen!

3. Taliban take over: The withdrawal of the international forces is seen a victory by the Taliban and regional spoilers. Taliban would feel motivated and enhance their fights to take over. This would follow new, but continued, rounds of intensive fighting. It would be of course a worst case scenario with a lesser chance to happen, as Afghanistan once again becomes a hub for terrorist and fundamental groups threatening peace and stability at the regional and international levels.[3]

The Afghan Government Initiative for Peace and Reconciliation

- Afghan government convened a 'Peace Consultative Jirga' to discuss ways forward for a political settlement. In June 2010, it brought about 1600 Afghans to work on feasible measures to establish contacts and negotiate with Taliban. There were lots of controversies about the composition of the 'Jirga' members, as they were seen as handpicked, with much known political affiliation and sympathy to Afghan government rather than being committed to peace and reconciliation with the Taliban.

  By and large, in the Jirga there was a consensus to promote negotiation with Taliban, while keeping military pressure on them and focus on 'Good Governance', reform judiciary, enhance fight on corruption and speed up merit-based appointment and meritocracy.

  Eventually, it led to establishment of a High Peace Council (HPC), as a national entity, in 2011 with 70 members (9 women, at least two were representing civil society and women's groups) with a diverse background. Some former Taliban members, Jehadi leaders, scholars, MPs and Senators were included as members of the PHC to promote reconciliation efforts with Taliban and other insurgent groups. In the absence of clear strategy, the HPC lost its head, Prof. Rabbani, as well as many of their members at the provincial level in its hectic effort to meet so-called high rank Taliban officials[4].
- Meanwhile, various initiatives were taking place at various levels. Everyone from the international community wanted to take precedence from others in finding a way to negotiate with Taliban. The US, UK, Norway, Germany, and some Gulf countries, with some initiatives by the UN special representative, though not publicly, wanted to reach to Taliban. All these talks bore no fruition, but made the Taliban very much in Demand, while systematically overshadowing the Afghan government's efforts!
- There was, on the other hand, no willingness from the Taliban towards any negotiation with the Afghan Government that was keen to advocate for an 'Afghan-led, and Afghan-owned' peace process! Those elements of Taliban, who were keen to enter into cycle of negotiation with the Afghan government, were arrested by Pakistan authorities. Apparently Pakistan doesn't want to lose control over Taliban and the peace process with them.

- Rumors were coming out about a meeting in Dubai, Germany, Norway, and elsewhere between Taliban, Americans, and elements of Afghan political opposition groups. This was a bit upsetting by PHC and the Afghan government, as they see themselves bypassed, somehow intentionally.
- Nonetheless, in 2012 the PHC was able to prepare a controversial road map for peace with Taliban, which was shared to the government of Pakistan at a meeting in Istanbul seeking their support and collaboration. The document was emphasizing three red lines: (1) accepting the Afghanistan Constitution; (2) renouncing violence, and; (3) cutting ties with Al-Qaida and any international terrorist groups. So far no any further elaboration about this took place.
- The PHC had various trips to Pakistan, Turkey, Saudi Arabia, Maldives, and Gulf countries. The outcomes of these trips were not made public, and are still not clear. It is why people are suspicious of such behind the scene activities, and seeing all these efforts as political compromises rather than genuine peace talks!

Civil Society, Rights Groups and Women's Groups Concern

- Civil society advocates and activists were against the essence of negotiation with Taliban. But they say the negotiations should be very value-based and principle-oriented in upholding human rights, women's rights, freedom of expression, as well as the gains made through the last decade.
- Civil society and rights groups raised their voices through a resolution to Bonn-II conference in December 2011. Promisingly some points were included in the final Communiqué of the Bonn-Conference. The CSOs were urging the Afghan Government, as well as the international community to:
  - Uphold core human rights values in any further peace talks with Taliban and any other groups,
  - No compromise on women's rights and the gains made in the last decade,
  - Chalk out a comprehensive and transparent policy for negotiation with full engagement of Afghan people and particularly victims and women,

- Monitor the process (and based on lessons learned from the past) of reconciliation and particularly reintegration of former Taliban or Hezb-e-Islami combatants.

The Notion of Afghan-led and Afghan-owned Peace and Reconciliation Process

- This is very ideal to have such an Afghan-led and Afghan-owned process for peace and reconciliation.[5] But practically it has various implications:
  - It would systematically overshadow the regional and international aspects of the problem in Afghanistan, as it is not solely an Afghan issue, but an issue with regional and international dimensions,
  - It would smartly cover the invisible hands of regional spoilers in supporting Taliban and insurgency in Afghanistan, while turning the table in favor of interested proxy groups.
  - As one critic was saying 'Afghans are good fighters, but not good negotiators', it is therefore needed to promote a principle-based negotiation based on clear and transparent strategy for peace protecting the gains of the last decade through a third party, who is well accepted to carry a role of mediator or facilitator along Afghans,
  - Overemphasis on this notion would systematically further blur the missing role of an international mediator, e.g., the UN.

The notion of 'Afghan-led and Afghan-owned' peace process would only work, when efforts at the national, regional and international levels are well coordinated. For sure interaction of efforts at these three levels would bear an expected and desired outcome, immediately for Afghanistan and in long-run for the region:

At the national level: The Afghan government needs to effectively strengthening 'good governance' and promoting constitutional political order, demonstrating strong political will in curbing corruption and supporting meritocracy in all official appointments, and to ensure people's access to justice, while putting an end to impunity.

At the regional level: The regional countries are willing to revisit their narratives for regional peace and stability, as well as national interest and sovereignty; to support and cooperate for peace in Afghanistan, and; to work towards addressing the root causes of extremism in the region; and to enhance economic and commercial cooperation at the regional level through existing mechanisms such as SAARC[6], RECCA[7], Shanghai, and OIC[8]. Finally the regional countries are willing to effectively join hands to introduce a new South Asian identity for peace and stability at the regional and global levels,

At the international level: The international community would maintain its long-term commitment and support for effective 'nation-building' and 'state-building' process in Afghanistan and enhances its efforts to promote democracy and human rights in the region, and the timely engagement of the UN to play its mediatory task to complement the so called 'Afghan-led and Afghan-owned' peace process.

The 'Afghan-led' and 'Afghan-owned' initiative must be supported at the national, regional and international levels.

END NOTES

1. Hezb-e-Islami's leader Gulbodding Hekmatyar has announced that he would allow and urge his party members to take part in the elections in 2014. What a surprise!
2. Regarding the outcome of the presidential election there will be various scenarios ranging from a first round winner to a second round winner or coalition of two top runners in the second round to coalition of many candidates to a so-called coalition government or broad-based government (similar to Bonn-I conference outcome) are anticipated. However, it very much depends on maturity of political coalitions and willingness of the Afghan government not to meddle in the process! Current stubborn stance taken by President Karzai regarding Bilateral Security Agreement (BSA), somehow, shows his keen interest in maintaining his grip to power.
3. There are various reasons for this not to happen: 1) Pakistan is facing growing threats from radicalisation and Talibanisation, on the other hand the economic condition of Pakistan would not allow them to extend their support to Taliban; 2) there is no open support to Taliban by regional countries and international community; 3) People are not willing to once again experience Taliban's harsh rule; 4) Now the social mosaic of Afghan society is different from what it was during four decades back, as now people are more interested in their children, particularly girls', education, and; 5) people's connectivity as well as the country's connectivity to the world and particularly to region would make it very challenging for Taliban to rule the country the way they wish. Interestingly some hardline Taliban has now established their private schools and university for girls' higher education – e.g., Mullah Salaam Zaeef, Mawlawi Motawakil, who are now in Kabul.
4. In the absence of a clear understanding on who might be a high rank Taliban official, and inadequate coordination amongst ANSF, an ordinary shopkeeper from Quetta pretended to be Mullah Mansoor managed to shake hand with the president and then to disappear with bags of money!
5. Ideally the 'Afghan-led' and 'Afghan-owned' process would only work when there are: (1)

Strong political will; (2) Capacity among Afghan stakeholders, and; (3) Professionalism. In the current situation all such initiatives are prone to political and ethnical manipulation and vulnerable to biasness and geographical affiliations!

6. Sadly SAARC is now hostage for India and Pakistan rivalry, and there is no much expectation out of it!

7. Regional Economic Cooperation Conference on Afghanistan with an overall objective to contribute towards sustainable growth in the region, especially in Afghanistan, by supporting tangible efforts at economic cooperation for mutual benefit throughout the region. RECCA was initiated in 2009 to follow-up the November 2006 New Delhi and 2005 Kabul conferences and their relevant suggestions for enhancing regional cooperation.

8. The Organisation of Islamic Cooperation (OIC) (formerly Organisation of the Islamic Conference) is the second largest inter-governmental organisation after the United Nations which has membership of 57 states spread over four continents.

3

Security and Development in Afghanistan after 2014

Wadir Safi

The UN Security Council resolution invited the intervention of the international community in Afghanistan after fall of Taliban in 2001. Despite a long history of the country, Afghanistan began its first steps toward development and security in the past decade. A country that needed to establish its very primary infrastructures for development with no economy had a long way to go and many initiatives to take. Through the international community's involvement, especially the NATO led operation, the progress towards development and security has taken place and the process is still ongoing. The war has not ended yet and development has not reached a level to meet people's needs.

The withdrawal of international forces, after 2014, will affect the progress and may cause other serious problems. The increase of instability and insecurity are not the only threats of Afghanistan after 2014. Loss of achievements of the past decade might be threatened. The region might be more unsafe after the withdrawal. Violence may increase and mass exodus of civilians for the fear of conflict may cause problems for international organisations and other countries. 2014 might be an alarm not only for neighboring countries but the UN and the world too.

Afghanistan still needs support of international community. UN and international community should continue their efforts for peace building and development. The role of UN should be enhanced and their strategies for development and security need to be improved.

Security

The general situation of country seems instable. Kabul, the capital, is the only province that people feel safe from war and military attack of Taliban. Suicide bombers are not the only threat for Kabul civilians; girls school poisoning, acid spreading and some other types of violations are the threat that makes Kabul insecure. The centers of many provinces are under control of the Government but not the entire province. Many districts in several provinces are ruled by Taliban. The Government does not have permanent presence in many districts. For instance, in Ghazni province, which is divided into 18 districts, only five to six districts are ruled by a government official district officer.

The national army which is formulated of 300,000 soldiers are not considered well trained but they have been patrolling around the country and borders. They rely on international assistance, mainly material to continue their operation. In many cases, the national army is considered to be unable to save the country from any outside attack.

The national police force, that majority of them is illiterate, provides security to government officials and secures Kabul from violence. National intelligence polices are present in many local structures and their duties are not clear; many civilians do not know if they have a role in the security section or not.

> At the current juncture Afghanistan is undergoing three defining transitions, which include the security transition from NATO-led ISAF to Afghan National Security Forces, a political transition that depends on negotiating a political settlement with the insurgency and upcoming presidential elections in 2014, and lastly the economic transition.

Afghanistan's ability to facilitate an effective economic transition will require, with the help of the international community, to leverage opportunities for cross-border commerce and people to people exchange.

Development: If we consider development as the progressive satisfaction of the needs of human and non human nature, starting with those most in need, I can say human needs in Afghanistan are not fulfilled. The growth of private sector is visible in many sides such as economy, education; health...To this effect, Afghanistan has already commenced infrastructural rehabilitation in all sectors whether it is railways, highways, energy sources, natural resource discoveries or trade and transit. Additionally, Afghanistan's neighbors in both South and Central Asia have also demonstrated, over the course of the last decade, their support for economic integration with various initiatives intended to advance regional economic cooperation.

Illustrative of some of achievements on part of the Afghan government membership in the various regional forums such as the Regional Economic Conference on Afghanistan (RECCA), the Economic Cooperation Organisation (ECO), South Asian Association of Regional Countries (SAARC) to name a few. Afghanistan has also become the central focus regional processes, such as the Istanbul Process, which was launched in 2011 together the countries surrounding Afghanistan including India, Pakistan, Tajikistan, Iran, Azerbaijan and China. This process recognised Afghanistan as the land bridge in the 'Heart of Asia' connecting South Asia, Central Asia, Eurasia and the East. The objective of the Istanbul process has been to promote regional security and cooperation to build confidence and trust among these countries while facilitating a stable and peaceful future for Afghanistan. Achievements of this process thus far including India's chairmanship of the working group focusing on expanding cross-commercial and business-to-business relations.

The transport, energy, and communication infrastructure working group is another critical initiative. Internationally, in October of 2012 Afghanistan in addition to other Central Asian Countries, participated in the U.S. Trade Representatives Central Asia Trade and Investment Framework Agreement (TIFA) council meeting which expands as alternative means to promote regional trade and cooperation.

TIFA agreement in 2004 that created a framework for dialogue between the two states issues related to development of trade and investment relations. Since 2001, the reconstruction efforts has focused significantly on building

Afghanistan's Association of Regional Countries (SAARC), and Shanghai Cooperation Organisations (SCO) to name a few. Afghanistan has also become the central focus of various regional processes, such as the Istanbul Process, which was launched in 2011 bringing together the countries surrounding Afghanistan including India, Pakistan, Tajikistan, Iran, Azerbaijan and China. This process recognised Afghanistan as the land bridge in the 'Heart of Asia' connecting South Asia, Central Asia, Eurasia and the Middle East. The objective of Istanbul process has been to promote regional security and cooperation to build confidence and trust among these countries while facilitating a secure, stable and peaceful future for Afghanistan. Achievements of this process thus far include India's chairmanship of the working group focusing on expanding cross-border commercial and business-to-business relations. While, Turkmenistan's chairmanship of a transport, energy, and communication infrastructure working group is another critical initiative.

Internationally, in October of 2012 Afghanistan in addition to other Central Asian countries, participated in the U.S. Trade Representatives Central Asia Trade and Investment Framework Agreement (TIFA) council meeting which explored alternative means to promote regional trade and cooperation.

Afghanistan is currently linked to Iran, Pakistan, Tajikistan, Turkmenistan and Uzbekistan through corridors established by the Ring Road (Kabul, Ghazni, Kandahar, Farah, Herat and Mazar) which is considered the longest route of the Asian Highway.

The Ring Road has the potential to play an important role in linking transit routes from Central Asia to the Persian Gulf and the Indian Ocean. There are 7 corridors on the Ring Road, which connects Afghanistan's provinces and some of its largest cities to the Asian Highway Networks of neighboring countries circumventing much of Afghanistan's rough terrain. The Ring Road is considered the backbone of Afghanistan's transport network and part of it is being built with the help of regional neighbors who are able to find markets for their goods in Central Asia and Iran.

- Private sector;
- Higher education;
- Education; and
- Health.

After 2014, it is feared that instability will increase (political, security and economy), opportunities may decrease (in several areas such as education and employment) displacement of people (mass number of people may leave the county) may increase thereby leading to the growth of threats for the region. There can be a spreading of insecurity to other neighboring countries and lack of assistance to maintain the operations will cause loss of control at the central levels, disable the operations and presence of national army and national police forces leading to human rights violations, increase of insurgent attacks and interventions of vested interest groups.

4

Afghan Migration 2014 and Beyond: A Regional Perspective

Anwesha Ghosh

Decades of conflict, war and serious human rights abuse have forced millions of men, women and children to flee from their homes and seek refuge in other parts of country or in foreign lands. Years of war profoundly shook Afghanistan and pushed a third of its population to exile, making them one of the world's largest conflict diasporas. While Afghanistan's population was dispersed among 72 different countries, 96 percent of these displaced Afghans resided in the neighbourhood, predominantly, Pakistan and Iran.[1] Afghan refugees have been subject of the largest repatriation undertaken since 2002, yet they continue to be one of the most protracted situations in the world. The role of migration in churning Afghanistan's demography and politics, both internal and regional, can hardly be exaggerated. The year 2014 marked a watershed for Afghanistan and the regional countries which host substantial Afghan refugee population. Series of assumptions and rough calculations have been underway to deal with the situation flowing from the inevitable drawdown of financial and technical assistance and the formidable challenges those developments might pose. Although there remains ambiguity about the final outcome of the political, economic and security transition in Afghanistan, what remains evident is that Afghan migration will continue to be one of the major issues to reconstruction within the post-2014 scenario.

Afghan Migration: A Quick Glance

Before dealing with the current migration environment in Afghanistan it is important to understand the particularities of the experiences and trends of the past. This article thereby, begins with a quick glance at the broad phases, which witnessed population movement in and out of Afghanistan. Although complex, Afghan migration contains some possibilities for categorisation, both in terms of phases and type of migration. Although the boundaries between the categories are porous and overlapping, this paper divides Afghan migration into four phases and identifies three broad types namely, elite migration, economic migration and conflict-induced migrations. The intention is not to describe each in details but simply to sketch out patterns against which one can consider the current and future trajectories.

Broadly, four phases can be identified which marked population movement out of Afghanistan:

Phase I (1979-88): For many Afghans the first escape out of Afghanistan took them to Pakistan and Iran, the two Muslim neighbours that opened borders to them.[2] These countries became home to one of the largest groups of refugee populations worldwide as approximately 6.2 million were displaced by the war following the Soviet intervention.[3]

Phase II (1989-1992): The withdrawal of Soviet troops from Afghanistan in 1989 caused a second and entirely new wave of population movements, both in (the return of those who had fled the Soviets) and out (the flight of many Soviet sympathizers) Afghanistan. The withdrawal resulted in an increase in the internal power struggle among the *mujahideen* groups.[4] This conflict in turn created two simultaneous migration movements: immigration into and emigration out of Afghanistan.[5] While many Afghan refugees (about 1.2 million) were encouraged to return following repatriation, others fled from the growing violence throughout the country.[6]

Phase III (1992-1996-2001): The next significant movement of Afghan population was witnessed between as a result of relentless internal conflicts between 1992-1996 and the Taliban regime up to 2001. The Taliban introduced a repressive regime with the "quest for a pure Islamic society",[7] and the political situation was exacerbated by a drought that created widespread food and water shortages throughout the 1990s. The persistent of violence and drought conditions meant that the state could no longer ensure adequate food, aid, or care for most of the population, particularly those residing in the countryside. During this period, an estimated 2 million Afghan refugees fled to Pakistan and about 1.5 million were forced to migrate to Iran. Others migrated to other countries in South Asia, the Middle East, North America, and Europe.[8]

Phase IV (2001-2012): This period witnessed a different kind of population movement at least initially when after several years in 2002, the region saw one of the largest return of refugees (more than 5.7 million) to their homeland as many Afghans made their journey back to the homes they had abandoned at the height of the war.[9] But a reverse flow was noticed following an escalation of Taliban insurgency since 2005. The repatriation of Afghans has declined fairly steadily over the last few years or so numbering about 68,000 in 2011 and 94,556 in 2012.[10] According to UNHCR, by the end of 2013 there was a 54 per cent reduction noticed in repatriation in comparison to 2012.[11] Subsequently with the declaration of 2014 deadline for the withdrawal of the NATO forces, a significant population movement is underway. The main countries of destination in the region have been Pakistan and Iran, where Afghans could feel closer to home for reasons ranging from geographical proximity, ethnic issues to religious affiliation. Yet some Afghans also fled to India, another country with longstanding relations with Afghanistan. Different factors triggered the decision to migrate to a foreign land however the following section briefly focuses on the conflict displaced Afghans in the neighbourhood countries namely Pakistan, Iran and India.

Conflict Displaced Migrants from Afghanistan in the Region

Pakistan and Iran have been the major hosts of Afghans for more than three decades. According to UNHCR data, as of 2013, over 1.6 million Afghans who are registered as refugees remain in Pakistan and an estimated 1 million more are unregistered. In Iran, more than 840,000 Afghan refugees are registered, and another 1 million or more live there unregistered.[12] In the initial phases, both the immediate Muslim neighbours of Afghanistan opened their respective borders to welcome the Afghan refugees not only because of the shared religio-ethnic and linguistic linkages but also because of the respect for the Afghan *Mujahid* who had fought *Jihad* against the Soviet infidels for the cause of Islam. However the enthusiasm was short lived and the refugee policies followed by both Iran and Pakistan underwent several changes based on internal and international politics as well as the size and duration of displacement. From a position of relative openness to and facilitation of refugee migration from Afghanistan (from late 1970s to 1988), their official policies went through a period of openness without facilitation (from around 1988 to 2001), to a posture of regulation and repatriation from 2001 onwards.

Although Pakistan did not sign the Geneva Convention or any other international conventions related to refugees like India, it recognised Afghans as 'refugees' and provided the registered refugees access to basic needs and necessities like food, shelter, education, health etc.[13] Pakistan received significant aid and assistance from international community to deal with the huge number of Afghan refugees who were primarily concentrated in the refugee camps and the neighbouring areas of the Pashtun dominated provinces of Khyber Pakhtunkhwa and FATA. The refugees belonging to Hazara ethnic group mostly concentrated in another bordering province, Baluchistan. During the 1980s, refugee camps in Pakistan provided significant support for the struggle against the forces of the Soviet Union and the Soviet-backed regime in Afghanistan.[14] The refugees proved an important asset in defeating the Soviet forces and later in the *Mujahidin*'s and *Taliban*'s successive efforts to conquer Kabul. But besides the larger strategic perspective which shaped Pakistan's Afghanistan policy (part of the country's India's policy, which falls outside the scope of the present study), the strategic management of the refugees by Pakistan's intelligence agencies had a rationale of its own, namely the 'Pashtunistan' issue, that is, the Pashtun claim to the Pakistani territories between the Afghan-Pakistan border and the Indus river.[15] Islamabad has pursued several parallel objectives in Afghanistan. First, it has been seeking to persuade the Pashtun refugees that Afghanistan, not a hypothetical Pashtunistan that would deprive Pakistan of a great deal of its own territory, is the country of the Pashtuns. Second and related, Islamabad has been trying to limit India's influence in Afghanistan in order to avoid the formation of an alliance between Afghanistan and India and the consequent risk of a two-front war with India should a conflict erupt. This has long been a feature of

Pakistan's Afghanistan policy.[16] Pakistan's various objectives did not necessarily contradict each other, but they influenced the state's perspective on the refugees, who were seen both as a potential strategic liability and also strategic assets. From Afghan refugee perspective however, they were being relegated to collateral damage of Pakistan's strategic constraints or ambitions. In the recent years, Afghan refugees in Pakistan have been at the receiving end of a hardened state policy. Provincial government authorities in the North West Frontier Province have been quoted in media reports as saying Afghan refugees are no longer welcome in Pakistan.[17] Pakistan's position, which stems from both social and economic concerns, cannot be taken lightly. However some research have also tried to indicate that Afghan labor migration could prove beneficial to Pakistan in the form of labor, and to Afghanistan in the form of remittances.[18]

Thirty years of war in Afghanistan has left Iran with a large urban refugee population in the world. Between 1979 and 2001, Afghan migration to Iran was primarily motivated by the direct and indirect effects of war, including widespread violence and insecurity, compulsory national service, insecurity, threat to female honour (*namoos*), unemployment and inflation.[19] The Soviet occupation of Afghanistan resulted in a massive influx of 2.9 million Afghans into Iran between 1980 and 1989. Based on estimates by the government of the Islamic Republic of Iran, the movement of Afghans into Iran continued at a slower pace to reach a peak of 3 million Afghans in Iran in 1991 before declining slowly until 2000 when an estimated 1.33 million Afghans remained in Iran.[20] More than 1.6 million Afghans have returned from Iran since April 2002, but the pace reduced significantly in 2006, with only around 5,000 returning due to lack of a better standard of living in Afghanistan.[21] The Iranian government's shift of attitude towards the Afghan refugees is apparent from the shift in terminologies used in formal literature to denote them. Afghans fleeing the Soviet invasion were initially greeted not as refugees or *panahandegan* but as 'involuntary religious migrants' or *mohajerin. Mohajerin* were given indefinite permission to reside in Iran and had access to free education and subsidized health care and food. Afghans were issued with identification cards known as "blue cards", and granted indefinite permission to stay in Iran.[22] While 80 camps or *mehmanshahr* were built, only about 2.5 per cent of the Afghan population in Iran resided in these camps; most Afghans settled in poor neighborhoods on the periphery of Iranian cities.[23] Since the mid 1990s the majority of new arrivals have remained undocumented. Afghans seeking refuge were no longer categorized as *Mohajerin* but as *Panahandegan*. Which basically indicated at the erosion of the element of honour attached with this population.

Unlike Pakistan, Iran ratified the 1951 Convention on Refugees and its 1967 Protocol, yet Afghan refugees living in Iran did not enjoy the international standard of uniform protection. In late 2001, the US military campaign in Afghanistan and subsequent fall of the Taliban saw Iran resolve to repatriate Afghans and prevent the entry of other Afghans by closing the border with Afghanistan. In January 2002, after installation of the internationally supported interim authority in Kabul, UNHCR shifted its programme in Iran to facilitate Afghan repatriation. The Tripartite Repatriation Agreement signed in April 2002 Agreement planned for the return of 400,000 refugees from Iran during the first year of operation, starting on 6 April 2002. It was estimated that the same number would return in 2003 and 2004.[24] In 2003, under Article 138 of the Constitution of the Islamic Republic of Iran, eleven articles were approved by Member Ministers of the Executive Co-ordination Council for Foreign Nationals. These eleven articles were titled "Regulations on accelerating repatriation of Afghan nationals".[25] Through these newly passes regulations it was rather obvious that the Iran government was no longer tolerant towards Afghans without valid documents for their stay in the country. It is also the backdrop against which a little over one million documented Afghans (1,009,354 individuals) remain in Iran including 190,765 households and 113,201 single Afghans,[26] and as many as 500,000 undocumented single Afghan labour migrants, some of whom move backward and forward between Afghanistan and Iran.[27]

The scale and speed of the return programme (particularly in the period March–September 2002 when 1.7 million Afghans returned from Iran and Pakistan) provoked discussion about the sustainable reintegration of Afghan returnees. Iran's economy has deteriorated since 2010. Among other indicators, daily oil production, the most important component of the Iranian economy, fell in September 2012 to the weakest level in 25 years.[28] The difficulties facing the Iranian economy is likely to filter into its decision to accept new refugees from Afghanistan in future.

It is difficult to estimate the exact number of Afghan refugees living in India as this depends largely on the 'refugee' definition being used.[29] Compared to Iran and Pakistan, the number of Afghans in India is much low. According to the recent data provided by UNHCR New Delhi, India hosts 10,442 refugees and 1,107 asylum seekers from Afghanistan mostly concentrated in and around New Delhi and belonging to religious minority groups.[30] A combination of structural failure and the rise of Islamic fundamentalist ideology in post-Soviet Afghanistan led to a war of ethnic cleansing after the Soviets left the country in 1989. Religious non-Muslim minorities like Sikhs and Hindus were systematically targeted, forcing many of them to flee Afghanistan.[31] Hindus and Sikhs found incentives to seek asylum in India, born of the ethnic and religious similarities to a segment of the Indian population. India has provided political asylums and hosted a section Afghan elites, however with the escalation of internal conflict in Afghanistan from 1992 and after 1996, when Taliban took over, common people from non-privileged backgrounds stared fleeing to India as an alternative to Iran and Pakistan. Though India has played a proactive role in reconstruction of Afghanistan by investing more than 2 billion dollars in its reconstruction process, it has relatively overlooked the plight of Afghans seeking refuge within its territory. The Indian government does not officially recognise the Afghan community to be refugees instead some of them are recognised and protected under the UNHCR mandate. This leaves the government to deal with Afghan refugees on an *ad hoc* basis. The Narendra Modi government in India reportedly granted citizenship to 4,300 Afghan and Pakistani refugees from Hindu and Sikh community in keeping with Bharatiya Janata Party's stated aim of positioning India as a 'natural home' for Hindus fleeing persecution anywhere in the world.[32] However such developments do not indicate much in terms of a well thought out refugee policy of the country. For several years now a need for structured refugee legislation in India has been acknowledged but so far nothing has been done in that regard.

Migration Scene: 2014 and Beyond

Despite systematic support over the past 14 years, Afghanistan's political and administrative institutions remained generally weak and frequently paralysed by corruption, turf battles and personal feuds.[33] Much of the available international analysis has focused on the impact of the withdrawal of international military forces from Afghanistan in 2014, the political transition resulting from the election of the new President Dr. Ashraf Ghani Ahmedzai will be just as important for security and stability in Afghanistan in the short-term. There are also concerns that an economic transition will reduce still further access to sustainable livelihoods for many Afghans, and this is likely to be just as important a driver for further migration as is insecurity. A cursory glance at the recent migration trend confirm that the need of assistance for displaced people are increasing at a time when the international and regional commitment to support humanitarian activities in Afghanistan are decreasing. Whereas Afghanistan is emerging from a period where aid was highly politicised and frequently militarised, ISAF withdrawal represents an opportunity to recast humanitarian action as impartial and independent. The next phase will be a period of limited financial means and diminished political attention from the western world, thereby extremely challenging for Afghanistan. These developments can be instructive in predicting future migration trends which can be applied to forecast the migration trends to neighbouring countries.

First, seeking asylum in Iran and Pakistan has become a survival strategy of which a significant proportion of the Afghan population already has either direct or indirect experience. Second, and a related point, is that many Afghans have family members or other relatives in Iran and Pakistan, on whom they may be able to rely should they decide to leave Afghanistan. Indeed, relying on informal support is likely to become increasingly significant as the government in both Iran and Pakistan reduce their welcome for Afghan refugees, and this declining hospitality is another factor that may influence the decision whether or not to leave Afghanistan.[34] Report published by International Organisation of Migration, however did not envisage massive new refugee flows to Iran or Pakistan citing two reasons.[35] First being that Pakistan and Iran have become less attractive places to seek work, in very recent years, as the opportunities available within the urban economy of Afghanistan have provided alternatives to the harsh treatment which Afghans may suffer in Iran and Pakistan. In the case of Pakistan, it has also been suggested that security concerns may put off potential migrants. It has been noted that Pakistan's own Pashtuns are currently moving away from Khyber

Pakhtunkhwa and the Federally Administered Tribal Areas because of insecurity, and these are the places traditionally that have absorbed largely Pashtun Afghan migrant and refugee populations. Specific mention has also been made of the situation of Hazaras who have become victims of targeted violence by Pakistan-based radical Sunni groups such as Lashkar-e-Janghvi.[36] In the west, potential refugees would need to continue to rely on irregular migration channels to access Iran. It is unlikely that the Iranian Government would make any provision to support such refugees, and may close its border. UNHCR has developed a Solutions Strategy for Afghan Refugees (SSAR), endorsed by the governments of Afghanistan, Iran, and Pakistan as well as donors, with a three-pronged approach of pursuing voluntary repatriation, supporting sustainable reintegration, and providing assistance to host countries, while maintaining a focus on the rights of refugees. While repatriation remains a priority, as indicated above numbers have dwindled, and forecasts as explained below are for even fewer returns during 2014.[37]

An elite exodus from Afghanistan has already been underway in anticipation of the transition, and is predicted to increase over the coming months. UNAMA Report expressed that individuals associated with, or perceived as supportive of, the Government and international community, including ISAF, are at risk of being targeted by anti-Government elements, especially in areas where these groups are active.[38] There has also been an increase in the number of Afghan refugees and migrants leaving Iran and Pakistan and heading for the West. In the region itself, India is likely to emerge as an alternative destination to Pakistan and Iran for Afghans. The relative positive image of India among Afghans coupled with the image of India as a stable and rising power in the region, is likely to make it one of the preferred destinations for Afghan immigrants. Afghanistan has bearing on India's security and economic interest. Post-2001, it provided India an opportunity to underscore its role as a regional power. India emerged as one of the major donor countries over the past decade reiterating its objective of touching lives of ordinary Afghans through developmental initiative. Talking about the plight of Afghans would hardly make little sense if Indian government chooses to ignore the plight of Afghans currently inside India.[39] It's time Indian Government considers implementing a structured refugee policy in order to deal with the immigration from its unstable neighbourhood.

To conclude, it can be said that in post-2014 Afghanistan, there is not only a risk of diverting attention and resources of the international community from those people already in need, but also of ignoring the impact of current and future developments on them. This paper, tried to provide a holistic perspective on the past and present migration scenarios and their impacts on Afghanistan's neighbourhood. It tried to explain the broad trends followed by the major host countries of the region in the past and also what their future positions could be vis-a-vis the migrants from Afghanistan. There can hardly be any doubt about the significance of the year 2014 certainly for Afghanistan's immediate prospects, as a result of security, political and economic transitions, which in turn will have displacement and migration implications. The paper particularly focused on Pakistan, Iran and India – which have considerable stakes in Afghanistan and are among the foremost countries in the neighbourhood and are likely to be affected by the developments in Afghanistan in the days to come. Although there are uncertainties pertaining to the exact approach they need to undertake to address the situation in Afghanistan, but it remains certain that migration from Afghanistan will continue to be the epicenter of humanitarian concern for the region.

END NOTES

1. Mamiko Saito, "From Disappointment to Hope: Transforming Experiences of Young Afghans Returning "Home" from Pakistan and Iran", *Afghanistan Research and Evaluation Unit Briefing Paper Series,* 2008.
2. L. Jazayery. "The migration-development nexus: Afghanistan case study". *International Migration,* Vol. 40, (2002), pp. 231-252.
3. "Afghanistan 10 years after Soviet pull out." *The UNHCR Briefing Notes,* 12 Feb, 1999. Available at http://www.unhcr.org/cgi-bin/texis/vtx/search?page=search&docid=3ae6b81cf0&query=Return%20to%20Afghanistan (accessed on 19.7.2015)
4. L. Jazayery. "The migration-development nexus: Afghanistan case study". *International Migration,* Vol. 40, (2002), 239.
5. R. Mandel. "Perceived security threat and the global refugee crisis". *Armed Forces and Society,* Vol. 24, (1997) p.89.
6. Ritendra Tamang, "Afghan Forced Migration: Reaffirmation, Redefinition and the Politics of Aid". *Asian Social Science,* Vol. 5, (2009), pp.3-12
7. S. Schmeidl, "(Human) Security Dilemmas: Long-term Implications of the Afghan Refugee Crisis." *Third World Quarterly,* Vol. 23 (2002), pp.7-29.
8. Ibid, p. 18
9. Aidan O'Leary, "2014 and beyond: implications for displacement". *Forced Migration Review,* Vol.46, (2014). p.4.

10. UNHCR Afghanistan, "Conflict-induced internal Displacement, Monthly Update",(2013), May.
11. UNHCR Afghanistan, "VolRep and Border Monitoring Monthly Update", (2013), November.
12. "Pakistan Global Appeal 2014-2015", *UNHCR,* Vol.1, 2014. Available at: http:// www.unhcr.org/528a0a300.html. See also Norwegian Refugee Council, NRC Pakistan – Fact Sheet (2013), 1, http://www.nrc.no/ arch/_img/9687894.pdf. (accessed on 19.7.2015).
13. S.G. Khattak, "Insecurity: Afghan refugees and politics in Pakistan". *Critical Asian Studies,* 35, (2003), pp 195–208.
14. Fiona Terry, *Condemned to Repeat?: The Paradox of Humanitarian Action* (Ithaca: Cornell University Press, 2002), pp. 55–82; Sarah Kenyon Lischer, *Dangerous Sanctuaries? Refugee Camps, Civil War, and the Dilemmas of Humanitarian Aid* (Ithaca: Cornell University Press, 2005), pp. 44–72.
15. Stanley Wolpert, *Roots of Confrontation in South Asia: Afghanistan, Pakistan, India, and the Superpowers* (New York: Oxford University Press, 1982), p. 120.
16. Frédéric Grare, *Pakistan and the Afghan Conflict 1979–1985* (Karachi: Oxford University Press, 2003), pp. 9-17.
17. Zulfiqar Ali, "More Afghan Refugees Not Welcome: Minister". *The Dawn,* October 26, 2013. http://www.dawn.com/news/1051934.
18. Rhoda Margesson, "Afghan Refugees: Current Status and Future Prospects" Congressional Research Service, Washington, 2007.
19. M.J. Abbasi-Shavazi and D. Glazebrook, "Continued Protection, Sustainable Reintegration: Afghan Refugees and Migrants in Iran", *Afghanistan Research and Evaluation Unit* (2006), 3.
20. "2013 UNHCR Country Operations Profile - Islamic Republic of Iran", http:// www.unhcr.org/cgi-bin/texis/vtx/page?page=49e486f96&submit=Go
21. M.J. Abbasi-shavazi et al, "Return to Afghanistan? A study of Afghans living in Mashhad", *Afghanistan Research and Evaluation Unit,* (2005), available at: http://www.areu.org.af/ Uploads/Editionpdfs/527E-Afghans%20living%20in%20mashad-Cs-web.pdf (accessed on 19.7.2015).
22. Alessandro Monsutti, "Afghan Transnational Networks: Looking beyond Repatriation", *Afghanistan Research and Evaluation Unit,* Kabul, August 2006, p.13.
23. Mohammad Jalal Abbasi-Shavazi, Glazebrook, Jamshidiha, et. al., "Return to Afghanistan? A Study of Afghans Living in Tehran", *Afghanistan Research and Evaluation Unit,* Kabul, June 2005.
24. D. Turton and P. Marsden, "Taking Refugees for a Ride? The Politics of Refugee Return to Afghanistan," *Afghanistan Research and Evaluation Unit,*(2002) p. 19.
25. Alessandro Monsutti, " Afghan Migratory Strategies and Three Solutions to the Refugee Problem". *Refugee Survey Quarterly,* (2008), pp.1-16.
26. Afghan population and family status in Iran as of 1 November 2004, Amayesh and Repatriation databases (note: there are some missing data values in the source) in Mohammad Jalal Abbasi-Shavazi, Glazebrook, Jamshidiha, et. al, "Return to Afghanistan? A Study of Afghans Living in Zahedan", *Afghanistan Research and Evaluation Unit,* Kabul, October 2005.
27. US Committee for Refugees, *World Refugee Survey 2004 Country Report.* Available at http:/ /www.refugees.org/countryreports.aspx?subm=&ssm=&cid=118 (accessed on 22.7.2015)
28. R. Gladstone, "Data on Iran Dims Outlook for Economy", *The New York Times,* 12 October

2012, Available at.http://www.nytimes.com/2012/10/13/world/middleeast/data-on-iran-dims-outlook-for-economy.html?_r=0 (accessed on 21.7.2015)

29. Shuchita Mehta (Senior Communication / Public Information Assistant, UNHCR India) in discussion with Anwesha Ghosh, October 2014.
30. Jayant Sriram, "4,300 Hindu, Sikh refugees from Pakistan, Afghanistan get citizenship". *The Hindu,* June 15, 2015.
31. Aidan O'Leary, "2014 and beyond: implications for displacement". *Forced Migration Review,* Vol. 46, (2014), p.4.
32. Khalid Koser, "Transition, Crisis and Mobility in Afghanistan: Rhetoric and Reality", *International Organization for Migration,* (2014) p.18.
33. Ibid.
34. Malik Ayub Sumbal, "The Plight of the Hazaras in Pakistan". *The Diplomat,* July 4, 2013.
35. UNHCR Afghanistan. *Solutions Strategy for Afghan Refugees Summary Progress Report,* September (2013). Available at :http://www.unhcr.org/pages/4f9016576.html (accessed on 22.7.2015).
36. UNAMA Afghanistan. "Protection of Civilians in Armed Conflict", *UNAMA Annual Report,* (2012). Available at http://unama.unmissions.org/LinkClick.aspx?fileticket=K0B5RL2XYcU%3D (accessed on 22.7.2015).
37. Anwesha Ghosh, '"Post 2014 Afghanistan: India's Interests and Concerns", Centre for Land Warfare Studies (CLAWS), January 2014, New Delhi, India. Available at: www.claws.in/Post-2014-Afghanistan-Indias-Interests-and-Concerns-Anwesha-Ghosh.html(accessed on 22.7.2015).

5

Democratic Transition in Afghanistan and Popular Reflections

Chayanika Saxena

Unlike what the conventional wisdom of the post-9/11 era would suggest, Afghanistan's dabbles with democracy are not so new. Not an age-old quest either, however the so called 'dawn of democracy' in Afghanistan in the 21st century maintains antecedents in the attempts that were made to democratize the country back in the 1950s.[1] Right from the reign of what was to be the last in the monarchical order in Afghanistan, the steps towards unfurling of democracy were begun being taken in whatever (wanting) measures under *Zahir Shah*. *Mohammad Daoud* who declared the country a Republic for the first time in its history continued to tread on the path of democracy, however deficient it was. The rise of the Peoples' Democratic Party of Afghanistan (PDPA), which ultimately avalanched into the Communist takeover of the country, was very much an embodiment of the democratic drive that was slowly taking the grip of the main, urbane political centers of Afghanistan.

However, even as the Afghanistan of today may not be charting an entirely unknown and new territory, the current democratic transition in the country is being performed in the background of a rather unsuccessful past. Besides the democratic flirtations going wrong, the unbridled political chaos that punctuated the *democracy-of-then* and the *democracy-of-now* weighs heavily on the expectations about the present democratic experiments, and of course, on their fulfillment. Added to this, an ever-present and increasing international pressure to make democracy a success in Afghanistan is breathing down the neck of this fledgling attempt.

It is in the background of the heightening domestic and international expectations from the current democratic attempt and an equally heavy baggage of a dismal and not so distant past that this paper will locate its inquiry around its central question: *how has democracy fared in Afghanistan?* Reflecting on the democratic transition that is currently underway in Afghanistan, this paper will explore the popular sentiments that thrive vis-à-vis this political development, with the views from the *Afghan Pathans* of Kolkata adding some expatriate insights into it.

The Trajectory of Democracy

'I have been in India for the last 35 years and have not seen the face of my land ever since; what do you want me to tell you about the politics of my country?' said one of the respondents at a (small) gathering[2] of the *Kabuliwalas* who I had the chance of conversing[3] with for this paper. The initial reluctance to speak about the politics of *their land* slowly gave way to an active interest in trying to fathom the politics of a country that has confused the domestic constituencies and the international spectators alike, and for one queer reason: *its sheer unpredictability*.

Like most of the countries across the world, Afghanistan has had its share of experiences with myriad models of political governance since its inception. From the rule of monarchy that changed hands between two major (Pashtun) clans—Sadozai and Barakzai to a limited monarchical rule, to a (somewhat) democratic Republic, to anarchy and political chaos and extreme repression, and finally democracy, Afghanistan has trodden its political journey on the tangents than on a clear, central path that it had envisioned for itself.

The political volatility and fluctuations in Afghanistan also meant that the domestic constituencies within the country were confounded about the political orders that presided over them from time to time. The same confusion persists in the evaluation of the political regime that exists in Afghanistan, or at least, is being attempted to be established in the current date—and, which is democracy. While not fully unaware—for reasons that include both the previous experiments with democracy as also the (tribal) operations among the (majority ethnic) population of Afghanistan (Pashtun) that stressed on popular participation—democracy in its western avatar came to the people of this country as a puzzling entity.

In fact, capturing the *bewilderment* of the Afghans towards a model of governance that stood the least for its much touted motto—*of the people, by the people and for the people*—Arbabzadah compiled the reactions of the common-folk towards this western political dosage.

> Democracy did not come cheap, but in a country where humans were forced to live in caves, for a want of a roof over their heads, the electoral pomp did seem morally questionable to some.[4]

Added to which,

> With little to zero understanding of the way democracy works in developed countries, a majority of Afghans failed to grasp (it)... After all, until their recent history, Afghans had only been exposed to invasions by the Soviet Union and Al-Qaida, an authoritarian regime and a dictatorial shadow state respectively, each with their coherent policies based on dogmatic ideologies. An intervention led by a host of democratic societies with pressure groups, political parties, lobby groups and powerful media vying to shape public opinion and policy was new and bewildering to Afghans.[5]

Likened to many Third World countries, Afghanistan too began its journey on the path of democracy on a largely illiterate popular base. In fact, even as we speak today, the Afghan society does not comprise of more than 28.1%[6] of literate population. But, while the linkages between democracy and literacy are well explicated, often to indicate a positive, proportional relationship between them, the lack of literacy in Afghanistan does not translate into lack of interest in politics within the society. In fact, the political history of the many ethnicities in Afghanistan would come to speak of an intricate association of social life with aspects of political governance. In this light, the democratic transitions of today have invited deep interest in the society, albeit of kinds that range from conscious, alert participation to distant viewing to outright admonishment of the process.

If the past is allowed to reside where it belongs, and which is *the past*, the democracy of today in Afghanistan was inaugurated after a hiatus of almost thirty-years of political chaos, anarchy (of the Civil War) and organised repression (of the Taliban era). It was with the Bonn Agreement[7] 2001 that the *era of political transition* was heralded in the country, marking a collective (international-domestic) attempt to change-over from the political orders (or, the lack of it) of the past to a kind of semblance that was more in sync with the Westphalian standards. The intention of the Bonn Agreement was to provide the political class in Afghanistan something to chew on, i.e., an initial plan of action, while also giving it time to gather domestic support for a future democratic course that its international benefactors wanted it to tread.

In fact, the major landmarks envisaged and accomplished as under the Bonn Agreement can be highlighted as follows:

> establishment of the 'transitional government' (under the leadership of *Hamid Karzai*) at the Emergency *Loya Jirga* in 2002 and the ratification of a new Constitution at the Constitutional *Loya Jirga* eighteen months later… the election of a President in 2004, and finally, the holding of the Parliamentary and Provincial Council Elections in 2005.[8]

However wanting they may have appeared to both the international spectators and the domestic participants, the attempts made at transitioning to democracy in Afghanistan were a welcomed development. The transition to a sustainable model of democratic governance appeared to be in the offing, only to be weighed down by exceeding popular expectations and even higher rate of political corruption. There still exists a very 'notional understanding of democracy'[9] in Afghanistan, which is fueled in equal proportions by a domestic audience that is not aware of the dynamics of democracy; the international pressure, and finally, those foreign-bred Afghans who are returning to their country, or are at least, wanting to see their country function in a manner that resembles the mature democracies of the West.

The 2004 elections were followed by another round of Presidential elections in 2009, in which *Hamid Karzai* became the President of the Islamic Republic of Afghanistan yet again. Plagued with allegations of corruption, a very low turn-out and a persistent threat by the Taliban, the commitments to democracy that were eagerly undertaken at the time of the Bonn Agreement appeared to be falling by the way-side. The clauses in the Preamble and Article 6 in the Constitution of Afghanistan[10], and even the Afghanistan National Development Strategy[11] that was the brain-child of the first president of the Islamic Republic (of the 21st century Afghanistan) were shown no ardent obedience and observance, resulting in the erosion of popular faith in democracy in the country.

It is equally crucial to note that the inaccessible terrains that are dotted by even more inaccessible (tribal) communities have been responsible for ineffectual state-control emanating from the center in Afghanistan. Fed into it is the *myth of independence* that makes centralised control in the country at best, resisted and at worst, abominable. As explained by Arbabzadah, there exist *varieties* of political orderings in Afghanistan, each of which claim to an *aura of legitimacy*

> Depending on exactly which part of Afghanistan you are, you are bound to encounter a different political system in action... The official government and its ghost mini-rival regimes co-exist in a geographical space where presidential elections are held every five years.[12]

Called the *graveyard of empires,*[13] Afghanistan has come to believe in its ability to duck any kind of centralised subservience, be it the empire (Britain) and the superpower (Soviet Union) that ruled it, or for that matter, its own centralised state-structure.

> (This) myth (of independence) was the narrative upon which the Afghan state was founded in the late nineteenth century... But, the myth of independence is a double-edged sword that can be turned against foreign invaders and legitimate local governments alike. When turned against local governments, the myth of the Afghan's natural right to independence turns into a license to riot and rebel without any sense of wrong doing.[14]

A combination of this 'free spirit', with a political class that is mired in corruption and an incessant threat to the security of the common people robs democracy off the kind of charm that is cherished in the Western world to the greatest extent. The recently concluded elections of 2014 were a tell-tale of these very dismaying factors that have affected the credibility of democracy in Afghanistan. In fact, if the pre-election, during-election and post-elections scramble-for-power is anything to go by, then the country still appears to be fractured along ethnic lines which are being accentuated further by the regional leaders and their financially and militarily powerful coteries.

Quest for Stability or Struggle for Power?

The 2014 run-off between *Dr. Ashraf Ghani Ahmadzai*[15] and *Dr. Abdullah Abdullah*[16] was fraught with troubles of all kinds. Being conducted in the year that was staring at the imminent draw-down of the US forces, the Presidential elections were marked by inter-ethnic clashes, allegations of colossal corruption and disenchantment on both the sides of the political camps and the social constituencies which they claim to represent. The present government that is installed in Afghanistan, which goes by the name of *National Unity Government*, stands the least for its name. A compromise-government of sorts that sought to placate the various claims to legitimacy, the political order at the center in Afghanistan is as fractious as the country appears to be. The Cabinet is far from being complete, with a Taliban that is being resuscitated by the political vacuum over vast-lands of Afghanistan creating troubles for this nascent democracy. Thus, not only the first, but the subsequent impressions of democracy in Afghanistan too succeeded little in charming the domestic populace, let alone the *mature democratic* benefactors of the West.

The situation as it stands today speaks of thorough disappointment with what was expected of the democratic order. While witnessing a moderate participation (38.90%)[17], the elections of 2014 could not glide over the internecine struggles within Afghanistan, with the consequence being that the electorate still remains divided in support on the basis of ethnicity (as a major factor among other aspects)[18]. In fact, as pointed by Arbabzadah, the dominance of ethnicity continues unfazed in Afghanistan and so much so that:

> for some critics, the race between Karzai and Ghani (and the ultimate transition from the rule of the former to the latter) is no mark of progress and only a continuation of the old tribal rivalry of Durrani versus Ghilzai Pashtuns for the leadership of Afghanistan.[19]

While affected by persistent squabbles for control between the centrally-placed claimants of authority, the seat of central power of Afghanistan finds itself further assaulted by a scramble-for-possession by the regional political elites. The struggle-for-Kabul is aggravated by the demands that are kept on it by the keepers of regional political authorities in Afghanistan, which carve the country into 3 broad zones: North centered on Mazar-i-Sharif; South centered on Kandahar and West, with its center around the province of Herat.[20]

However, this 'federal' struggle, which could otherwise have been celebratory for being a measure against any impulse for extreme centralisation of power, is far from being a manifestation of this healthy check-and-balance relationship. The regional political niches that have been carved throughout the country are exhibiting what I call are *centripetally-centrifugal tendencies*[21]—where, there is a constant rush to occupy the center, but not with the intention of consolidation but for the purpose of strengthening one's position back in their regional basis.

Appearing to be a loose confederation of sorts that is sticking together more for the sake of convenience (and other factors that have got less to do with 'national consciousness')[22], the Afghanistan of today finds itself dealing with other set of security issues that are both indigenous and exogenous to it. The revival of the Taliban aside, an ostensibly increasing presence of the forces of the Islamic State of Iraq and Syria (ISIS) is eating into the domestic constituencies of the former, making the struggle for power even bitter in Afghanistan. And, in all of this, it is Afghanistan's trust in a centralised, democratic government that is emerging as the biggest casualty.

Afghans, but quite not: Afghan Pathans of Kolkata

Witnesses to the political volatility of their country—albeit from outside—the Afghan diaspora in Kolkata finds itself to be a distant, but not a removed audience from all that is transpiring in Afghanistan and in the respective provinces to which they belonged. The democratic transitions and the governments that have been installed since 2001 have been carefully observed, and even dissected, and continue to be subjected to their critical evaluations.

Like many of their Afghan and international counterparts, the Afghans of Kolkata too have witnessed a shift in their perception of democracy—one, which changed from extreme optimism, to cautious optimism to the lack of faith in its efficacy as the first decade since the transition rolled by. The tense and uncertain, or rather, unpredictable political situation in Afghanistan which is being compounded by intensifying assaults to domestic security has added to the disenchantment of those who had hoped to go back to their home, astride on their trust in the potency of democracy. But, the fate of the democratic order as it stands today hardly seems disposed to grant them their wish.

The Afghan diaspora in Kolkata is predominantly from the ethnic community of Pashtuns and has its origins in the southern states of Afghanistan. While not a monolithic community, the Pashtuns, or who are colloquially referred to as *Pathans*, this community of expatriates originates in that regional sphere of Afghanistan that has been the progenitor of both rule and chaos in the country. The royal-tribal lineages of the monarchical past, as well as the recent memory of social, political and cultural repression of the Taliban found their agents originating in this part of the country. In fact, both the current President of the country as well as the former President too belong to the South of Afghanistan—the province of Logar and Kandahar, respectively.

Being at the forefront of politics in Afghanistan, the southern part of the country has been witness to an equal degree of political tumult. Infamously famous as the *badlands of Taliban*, the southern provinces to which most of the expatriate Afghan Pashtuns belong have been affected by insurgency and counter-insurgency operations, with little reach of the central government in these areas. As a result, the spread and efficacy of democratic models of participation have not been adequately felt.

'While I have not been to my country in the last 35 years, but it seems to be stuck in a time warp; a little has changed since then', said one of the respondents who is known in the *Chandni Chowk* in Kolkata by various aliases. As an Afghan expatriate from the province of *Ghazni*, this particular part of Afghanistan has been one of critical centers in the rise and fall of the medieval empires as well as the contemporary effort against the Taliban. What little has changed in this province, as the same respondent observers, 'are the hands of the exploiters—from Mujahedeen, to Taliban to those who claim to have popular, democratic mandate, and they do'.

Even as democracy was proclaimed as *the* political order in Afghanistan, the reality in Ghazni resonates little with what has been claimed. The same is true for two other provinces in the south, namely—*Paktia* and *Paktika.* Dismayed at the backwardness of their respective provinces even after a decade-long international 'adventure', the two *Hajis* from these two provinces spoke of how thankful they were to have arrived in India, 'than be stuck in that quagmire'. The province of *Khost* has the same story to tell, with its immediate contiguousness with the North Waziristan of Pakistan adding to the porosity of the borders, making cross-border movements of the 'fringe elements' possible and their elimination difficult.

The interactions between the four respondents, their yearning for their country and their frustration with the present state-of-affairs also threw up some of the recurrent themes in the politics of Afghanistan—*the regional and ethnic divide.* The respondents spoke in unison against the 'leaders in the north' who have been responsible for 'all the fractious ills' that have been plaguing the country. Calling 'mazaimat' (تمحازم)[23] in the creation of a 'unified Afghanistan', these leaders are believed to be the biggest obstruction in making the present government a success.

These leaders, who are *not* Pashtuns, are dismissed as trouble-mongers and trouble-creators for the present regime that is being run by a 'highly skillful' leader (Ghani). Steering clear of prognosis, calling it too premature, however, for them the stability of the present-day government is 'critically undermined by those who have been permitted into it'. As they spoke in cohesion, 'there are certain elements within the government that would not let Ghani work'.

Democracy; what about democracy? Not entirely dismissive of the process as they 'missed having not voted for the first time in their lives as Afghans', but they are not so hopeful about it either. With the fingers that were inked being chopped by the Taliban, they believe that an 'inked finger reminds them as much of the brutality that followed, but also of some freedom on the horizon'. But, given the provinces to which they belong, the execution of the democratic dynamics has not taken place beyond the conduct of polls, which were also mired in the charges of fraud and corruption.

As the international patience wanes and the domestic expectations are reaching a high, the situation in Afghanistan speaks of exasperation—disappointed with its own-self as well as with the world that is all-determined to 'pull itself out of this mess'.[24] This South Asian country is in need of continuous support that is both organically provided and exogenously pumped into it. The way ahead is tough, but it is not difficult to chart.

Miles to Go Before It Sleeps

As Robert Frost had rightly said, Afghanistan too has miles to cover before it can sleep. While recommendations to make the democratic order work in Afghanistan would take another paper, however, this attempt did try to delve into the multi-level issues that come to concern it. The process of rehabilitation of a war-weary society like that of Afghanistan would require a comprehensive effort, involving the (domestic) political and popular and international classes alike, and in which none should give up for the longest while.

Democracy as we see flourishing in the Western part of the world took centuries to become what it is today. The circumstances in the 21st century are a lot different, especially for a country that has spent the greatest part of the previous century in series of political turmoil. But, while the path seems to be tough, however, the age-long resilience of the Afghan population will enable them to get to the other side too. All that is needed is an undying collective action.

END NOTES

1. Saikal, 2004; Hopkins, 2012.
2. This paper shall not identify the respondents for the lack of requisite permission to reveal their identities. The length of our conversations and the lack of (adequate) familiarity, also the many aliases by which the respondents are known made it more logical and ethical to *not* to divulge the details of who they are. However, the place where this collective conversation took place was *Chandni Chowk* of Kolkata. The exact details of the location can be provided, if needed.
3. For their confident and comfortable command of Hindi, these conversations took place in the aforementioned language. Whatever sprinkles of Dari and Pashtu that were a part of the conversation were appropriately translated by my research partner, *Naser Rawan*. Special thanks to him for his active, voluntary service in making these conversations possible.
4. Arbabzadah, 2013, p. 202.
5. Ibid., p. 157.

6. For further information, refer to the information provided on the following website: http://www.indexmundi.com/afghanistan/literacy.html
7. The Bonn Agreement (2001) is officially known as '*Agreement on Provisional Arrangements in Afghanistan Pending the Re-Establishment of Permanent Government Institutions*'. The same can be accessed using the following link: http://www.un.org/News/dh/latest/afghan/afghan-agree.htm
8. Kippen, 2009, p. 35
9. Kippen, 2009
10. The (prevailing and latest) Constitution of Afghanistan can be accessed from here: http://moj.gov.af/en/page/1684
11. The document entitled, *Islamic Republic of Afghanistan: Afghanistan National Development Strategy (1387-1391),* envisages what Afghanistan of 2020 should be like. As a strategy document, it sets out goals that ought to be achieved in order to make Afghanistan a stable polity that is based on a strong society and the ways to achieve the same. The said Strategy document can be obtained using the following link: http://mfa.gov.af/Content/files/Volume%205%20ENG.pdf
12. Arbabzadah, 2013, p. 190.
13. Hopkins, 2012
14. Arbabzadah, 2013, pp. 150-151.
15. The profile of the (current) President of the Islamic Republic of Afghanistan can be accessed from here: http://president.gov.af/en/page/8262/8263
16. The profile of the Chief Executive Officer (akin to Prime Minister) of the Islamic Republic of Afghanistan can be obtained from here: http://ceo.gov.af/en/page/chief-executive-officer/biography
17. For further information on the statistics related to the Presidential Elections of 2014 in Afghanistan, the following source can be helpful. http://www.idea.int/vt/countryview.cfm?id=4
18. Exceptions to such an ethnically determined political loyalty are exhibited too, but they are by and large witnessed in minority. In fact, their relatively minuscule presence goes a long way to prove that the confluence between ethnicity and politics continues to writ large in Afghanistan.
19. Arbabzadah, 2013, p. 196.
20. Dorronsoro, 2005.
21. Saxena, 2015.
22. Dorronsoro, 2005.
23. A Farsi equivalent for the English word, 'disturbance'.
24. Arbabzadah, 2013.

REFERENCES

Arbabzadah, N. (2013). *Afghan Rumour Bazaar: Secret Sub-Cultures, Hidden Worlds and the Everyday Life of the Absurd.* London: C. Hurst & Co.

Dorrosnoro, G. (2005). *Revolution Unending: Afghanistan, 1979 to the Present (The CERI Series in Comparative Politics & International Studies).* New York: Columbia University Press.

Hopkins, B.D. (2012). *The Making of Modern Afghanistan (Cambridge Imperial and Post-Colonial Studies Series).* New York: Palgrave Macmillan.

Index Mundi (2014, August 23). *Afghan Literacy*. Retrieved June 27, 2015, from Index Mundi: http://www.indexmundi.com/afghanistan/literacy.html

International Institute for Democracy and Electoral Assistance (2014). *Voter Turnout Data for Afghanistan*. Retrieved June 27, 2015, from International Institute for Democracy and Electoral Assistance: http://www.idea.int/vt/countryview.cfm?id=4'

Kippen, G. (2009). *The Long Democratic Transition*. Retrieved June 27, 2015, from Ghosts of Alexander: Conflict and Society in Central Asia: http://easterncampaign.com/2009/01/13/the-future-of-afghanistan/

Ministry of Foreign Affairs, I.R. (2008). *Islamic Republic of Afghanistan: Afghanistan National Development Strategy (1387-1391)*. Retrieved June 27, 2015, from Ministry of Foreign Affairs, Islamic Republic of Afghanistan: http://mfa.gov.af/Content/files/Volume%205%20ENG.pdf

Ministry of Justice, I.R. (2004). *The Constitution of Afghanistan*. Retrieved June 27, 2015, from Ministry of Justice, Islamic Republic of Afghanistan: http://moj.gov.af/en/page/1684

Office of the President, I.R. (2015). *Biography of President Mohammad Ashraf Ghani*. Retrieved June 27, 2015, from Office of the President, Islamic Republic of Afghanistan: http://president.gov.af/en/page/8262/8263

Office of the Chief Executive, Islamic Republic of Afghanistan (2015). *Biography*. Retrieved June 27, 2015, from Office of the Chief Executive, Islamic Republic of Afghanistan: http://ceo.gov.af/en/page/chief-executive-officer/biography

Saikal, A. (2004). *Modern Afghanistan: A History of Struggle and Survival (First Edition)*. London: I.B. Tauris.

Saxena, C. (2015, February 24). *The Curious Case of Cabinet Formation in Afghanistan*. Retrieved June 27, 2015, from South Asia Monitor: http://southasiamonitor.org/detail.php?type=sl&nid=10795

United Nations (2001). *Agreement on Provisional Arrangements in Afghanistan Pending the Re-Establishment of Permanent Government Institutions*. Retrieved June 27, 2015, from United Nations: http://www.un.org/News/dh/latest/afghan/afghan-agree.htm

The Region and Afghanistan

6

Pakistan's Dilemmas in the Afghan Endgame

Ajay Darshan Behera

With the December 2014 deadline for the drawdown of foreign troops from Afghanistan, an uneasy transition in the Afghan end game seemed inevitable. At the beginning of 2014, it was not clear what will be the nature of this transition. The US followed a dual track in its withdrawal strategy. On one hand, it has supported a negotiated settlement in Afghanistan hoping to bring the Taliban on board. And on the other, it pursued a bilateral security agreement with President Karzai to seek guarantees for the planned residual force post-2014. While the contours of an exit strategy for US-NATO forces were put forward, it was difficult to comprehend how the endgame is likely to play out. Hopes of a negotiated settlement in the ongoing 13-year war look very bleak. Negotiations with the Taliban are unlikely to succeed. There are many other imponderables. The most important being—how does Pakistan view the endgame?

Fear is mounting that Afghanistan could fall into chaos following the pullout of most US-NATO combat troops by the end of 2014. There are two points of view doing the rounds regarding a post-2014 Afghanistan. One is an apprehension that the Taliban will run over Kabul once US-NATO forces withdraw from active combat. There is scepticism about the cohesiveness of the ANSF and whether it will have the strength to maintain security in all parts of Afghanistan. It is not clear whether it can withstand the Taliban or will fall apart. In case it falls apart, it will have grave implications for the stability of Afghanistan and the region. The other point of view is that we may not see a repeat of 1996 as the Taliban may not be as strong as some would like to believe and also is now pitted against a better-trained national army. It is possible that once the foreign combat troops leave Afghanistan, some Pashtun areas of Afghanistan may be re-conquered by the Taliban. Kabul may not fall to the Taliban. Both scenarios conjure a civil war like situation in Afghanistan and do not give much hope for stability in the short term.

Pakistan can play an important role in the Afghan endgame. Whether the Taliban weakens or strengthens has largely to do with Pakistan. It continues to be functional because of the sanctuaries in Pakistan and support of the Pakistan army. The leaders of the Taliban and the Haqqani network, its ally, have been holed up in Pakistan since fleeing Afghanistan in 2001. Even after joining the war on terror, Pakistan continued supporting the Taliban. Gen. Pervez Musharraf used the war on terrorism to perpetuate his own power. The prime minister of Pakistan, Nawaz Sharif, has however, said that Pakistan did not wish to intervene in Afghanistan in any way. Ostensibly Pakistan is backing the dialogue and supporting Western-backed attempts to engage with Taliban leaders. It has been playing an important role in bringing the Taliban to the negotiating table by releasing Afghan Taliban prisoners in its custody and urging them to play a role in the peace process.

Has there been a turnaround in Pakistan's policy on Afghanistan? Or has Pakistan kept all options open in the uncertainties of transition, backing dialogue partly due to fears that the end of the US-NATO combat mission in Afghanistan in 2014 could energise a resilient insurgency within Pakistan. It is not clear whether Islamabad is serious about promoting stability in Afghanistan or is merely making token moves to deflect Western criticism of Pakistan's record in Afghanistan. Many believe that Pakistan is keen to establish control over Kabul following the US-NATO force withdrawal scheduled by the end of this year. That it is still backing the Taliban in Afghanistan as a proxy force for a final settlement. The security narrative developed by Pakistan argues that it is justified in supporting the Taliban till Pakistan's security vis-à-vis India is taken care of.

But it is not clear to what extent it controls the Taliban. And there has been a blowback from Pakistan's policy of support for the Taliban. It has increased levels of violence in Pakistan. A lack of clarity on Pakistan's preferred outcomes from the reconciliation process do not convince observers that Pakistan means well. There is also a real possibility that Pakistan can be marginalised in the Afghan endgame. This is the dilemma confronting Pakistan. Unlike the 1990s, this time around Pakistan does not have much autonomy in deciding the outcome in Afghanistan. Unlike the 1990s, there is going to be no security vacuum in Kabul. A substantial presence of 8,000 to 12,000 troops in addition to the NATO contingent and contractors post-2014 is being discussed.

Further, Pakistan's internal difficulties do not also allow much space for an adventurist policy in Afghanistan. Pakistan's decision to support the war on terrorism has worsened its own security, dampened exports, reduced foreign investment, tourism and slowed privatisation. All that has led to lower tax revenue, bloated security expenditures, damage to infrastructure and huge costs to care for millions of Pakistanis who have fled the volatile tribal areas and become refugees in their own country. Many Pakistanis believe their government's complicated role in Afghanistan has worsened the plight of ordinary people. In an interview with Pakistan's *Dawn* newspaper, former Prime Minister Yousuf Raza Gilani said the war had cost Pakistan $ 68 billion. In the past 10 years, inflation has jumped from 4.4 per cent to 16 per cent, while Pakistan's national debt has climbed from $ 30 billion to $ 60 billion. Its average growth rate is 2.4 per cent and foreign exchange reserves have come down to $ 3 billion only.

A further prolonged conflict in Afghanistan, therefore, does not serve Pakistan's interests. It will give space to insurgent forces that are waging an anti-systemic fight in Pakistan. The longer the war goes on in Afghanistan, the stronger the Jihadi forces will become. The *Tehreek-e-Taliban Pakistan*, has declared that it is independent from the Afghan Taliban and is fighting for the implementation of Sharia Law in Pakistan and that they would continue to fight against the drone attacks, and Pakistan army and government, who are under the U.S. influence. The rise of the TTP has led to an existential struggle to save Pakistan itself from Talibanisation. Pakistan's military, has lost several thousand soldiers to these extremist groups. Over the last several years, the Pakistani government has engaged with the Pakistani Taliban groups in Waziristan, Swat, Dir, Bajaur, Mohmand and elsewhere. The Pakistan military has moved decisively against those militants that pose a direct challenge to its authority like in the main stronghold of the TTP in South Waziristan. But it continued to avoid military engagements that would put it in direct conflict with the Afghan Taliban, specifically the Haqqani network in North Waziristan.

Stability in Afghanistan is critical to Pakistan's security and development. Pakistan needs to be worried about the potential destabilisation of Afghanistan that could follow the US-NATO withdrawal. Possible results could include millions of new refugees if a civil war breaks out in Afghanistan and the scary prospect for Pakistan of reverse sanctuary for the TTP and other anti-state actors. US threats of a total withdrawal will also place enormous burdens on Pakistan. In the event of a civil war, a fresh influx of refugees from Afghanistan could stream across the borders into Pakistan. The security situation in the border areas would further worsen with the likelihood of the complete withdrawal of US aid.

Therefore, the continuing support for the Taliban despite the pressures suggests skewed national priorities. It is not clear to what extent Pakistan's strategic elites think that their muddled policy of supporting the Taliban has gravely compromised their security. But there are reasons to believe that Pakistan is unlikely to follow the policies of the 1990s. With a stronger democratic dispensation, the military's autonomy to decide policy on Afghanistan might also erode. Unlike the 1990s, the Pakistan military will also be under a great deal of scrutiny and will not find the manoeuvring space that it had in the 1990s. It will be faced with a serious dilemma in its inability to influence the outcome in the Afghan endgame.

7

Pakistan's Angst in Post-2014 Scenario

Maqsudul Hasan Nuri

Introduction

The post-2014 US/NATO military withdrawal from Afghanistan after eleven years is going to be a watershed event. The reactions on future outlook in Afghanistan are rather mixed—ranging from benign to the malign.[1]

The Afghanistan issue can be likened to Rubik's cube for its agonizing complexity: a three-dimensional puzzle with many permutations and combinations. This may seem too hyperbolic to state but the idea has some substance as any smooth, seamless transition after protracted conflict poses many challenges.

Barring an overly optimistic or downright calamitous outlook, the trends, as of to date, indicate that this changeover is going to be problematic and bumpy at least for the first five years or so—depending upon a host of factors: domestic, regional and global. More importantly, it also depends upon the role played by immediate and important eastern neighbour—Pakistan.

One is nonetheless tempted to list some positive scenarios that have taken place over the years in Afghanistan's polity: a Constitution has been framed; the third Afghan elections have taken place in April 2014; women representation is nearly 25 per cent; media and non-NGOs have developed a somewhat positive role and are trying to change the Afghan socio-cultural landscape; girl child education has registered remarkable growth; many Afghans have now access to outside world through digital communication and are relatively well informed; in security terms, the country can now boast of its own army and police—in all, nearly 8,50000 constituted. This positive view, also posits that a situation of 'pull and push' and jostling for influence by foreign powers changed and regional connectivity takes hold—thus making way for any regional cooperation. Hence, Afghan state is not totally dysfunctional. All these indicators reflect that the country is apparently morphing towards a semi-democratic polity but state institutions are still fragile and can relapse into semi-anarchy.

However notwithstanding these positive aspects, the question may be posed: Did the Soviet Union's military invasion (1979) and the US (2013) and subsequent attempts to usher social engineering and building democracy by US/NATO forces in the last 11 years accomplish much? Is neighbouring Pakistan after 12 general elections in its 67-year old history been able to change its feudal-tribal configuration? Has the legacy of "buffer" system established by then Russia and by Britain in the "Great Game" still repeatable or not?

Needless to say that with few exceptions Afghan politics remains predominantly feudalistic and tribal, where questions of honor, revenge and bloodshed dominate views of leadership at all levels. Besides, Afghanistan has developed a "rentier mentality" in history to play one rival against the other for financial rewards. It still lacks adequate infrastructure of roads and railways, judicial system and industry. While the socio-economic problems are galore, in this article, an attempt is made to highlight some of the major concerns of Pakistan after US/NATO military withdrawal by end of 2014.

Fresh Influx of Refugees

Pakistan has the longest border with Afghanistan and has absorbed the brunt of shocks since the events of 9/11: first, following the Soviet invasion (1979) and then the US military attack and occupation of Afghanistan (2001). As a "frontline ally" it has suffered immensely, incurring about 40,000 civilian casualties and martyrdom of 5,000 security personnel in the war against terror with a loss of nearly $70 billion. This count of human casualties and cost has mounted and may do so even after post-2014.

The biggest burden on Pakistan, however, has been the influx of refugees—the single largest refugee community in the last four decades. While nearly four million refugees streamed into Pakistan after the Soviet invasion (1979), presently about 2.7 million still reside in refugee camps out of which 1.07 million are registered with equally the same number as unregistered.[2] On humanitarian grounds, Pakistan has extended the date of return of the refugees till end of 2015. During the last 11 years, nearly 3.8 million left but many of them have come back to Pakistan due to adverse conditions and future uncertainty in Afghanistan. Pakistan's policy is the not to eject them by force but seek their voluntary repatriation. To help them, the government has extended some humanitarian gestures as nearly one million cannot avail some facilities; so, they were given some concessions like NADRA (identity cards) and facility of driving licenses.[3]

Pakistan has suffered heavily in economic terms due to the inflow of refugees: loss of jobs for the locals, inflow of unlicensed weapons, narcotics, militancy and terrorism from across the border.[4] Moreover, it has led to ethnic and sectarian tensions amongst different communities while they compete for jobs, housing, grazing land and water sources in tribal areas.

Pakistan has presently nearly 70,000-100,000 workers in Afghanistan and has annual formal trade of $1.2 billion with $800 million informal trade—cumulatively worth $2 billion in 2011.

Scheduled for a major military drawdown by end of December 2014 the US/ISAF forces may leave a murky situation in Afghanistan. Despite repeated assurance by the US the professional competence of Afghan National Forces (ANF) to grapple with future security the post-2014 situation many apprehensions persist.

An abiding concern is that in the post-2014 scenario, if internecine fighting erupts, the Afghan refugees' inflow in Khyber Paktunkhwa (K-P) province and further reaches of Pakistani mainland might take place, especially in urban centers. These urban centers are already becoming Pakistan's Achilles heel in spawning serious law and order issues in industrial hubs like Karachi.

The Durand Line remains porous and faces competing claims; frequent illegal crossings at different points continue as it is impossible to seal the border completely due to the rugged mountainous terrain. Nearly 100,000 people criss-cross the borders daily from various points. The Afghan government provides Pakistani Taliban haven from bases in eastern Afghan provinces of Kunar and Nuristan.

In fact, with the political transition since Nawaz Sharif came into power in since May 2013 the Taliban elements initially renewed their terrorist activities with greater vengeance and started mounting attacks to pressurise the government into submission by placing unrealistic demands i.e., release of all captured Taliban and criminals; withdrawal of Pakistani forces from the tribal belt; and enforcement of Islamic *Shariah* in Pakistan. A fresh round of talks was initiated in early in February 2014 but the prospects of success were dismal.

Should transition in Afghanistan turn bumpy and violent in post-2014 it may unleash fresh waves of refugees into Pakistan. Due to security issues in their own country the Afghans will continue to look abroad for protection, better education and jobs—and thus improve their economic status in face of diffused uncertainty.[5]

Further displacement of civilian population might occur after 2014 if conditions deteriorate. In case Afghan provincial cities fall into the hands of insurgents, dislocation of people, together with police and army breaking ranks to join civil population may also arise. Rise of new warlords and militancy could be a replay of 1990s pre-Taliban period. If skirmishes follow in south and eastern region of Af-Pak region then greater displacement could occur.[6] Economic deterioration and climate change effects are already contributing to this negative phenomenon. Although based on previous experience, Pakistan and Iran would try their best to limit the influx (Iran did much better than Pakistan through imposing strict restrictions) yet the long permeable borders could not prevent this leakage from happening.

Of greater concern to Pakistan, however, are the eastern Afghan provinces' refugees spilling into adjoining FATA. While 534,006 were recorded by UNHCR as displaced by conflict in Afghanistan, over 100,000 were displaced by internal conflict in Afghanistan in 2012 and further 32,000 by natural disasters.[7] But in case Afghanistan makes a smooth and peaceful transition this grim scenario could be mitigated.

Use of Drone Technology[8]

The US is relying on high technology to avoid own casualties by employing better intelligence, surveillance and fire power. Despite protests in Pakistan, it seems that drones, as an arsenal in US armory, may continue to be used in areas where militancy is rife, where national governments' writ is weak or lacks effective control—such as in Yemen, Somalia and FATA regions of Pakistan. But as a reaction, militancy and suicidal attacks have increased on Pakistani mainland and in big cities.

Pakistan has taken a stand against the use of drones in that they violate national sovereignty, cause civilian losses (civilian, women and children) and fuel militancy by igniting retaliatory suicidal attacks on Pakistani mainland. Even if they are precisely targeted and destroy high-value targets they cause "collateral" damage.

The US, on the other hand, often deploys the argument that since the Pakistani government lacks working consensus on how to deal with terrorism or has shown reluctance or incapability to deal with and eliminate the hideouts of terrorists. Ergo, the US is constrained to carry out them.

These drone attacks have killed some notable Al-Qaeda and some Taliban leaders during the last few years and thus demonstrated the utility of the weapon system. So far, since 2004, over 290 drone attacks have taken place killing combatants and civilians totaling almost 2,200.[9] Some Americans also claim that there was, and still is, an implicit understanding between the two militaries since General Musharraf's days.

As for the sovereignty principle, the Secretary of State John Kerry in his July 31 visit to Pakistan pointedly admonished by saying that Al-Qaeda Chief Al-Zawahiri, and TTP Chief Mullah Omer and other Afghan leaders were still lodged in Pakistani territory.[10] This was in addition to some foreign nationals ensconced in FATA.

Pakistani leaders and general public remain critical of the drone attacks. At times, they have advocated acquiring drone technology and shooting down of US drones by own air force. On other occasions, condemnation of the US policies is meant to shift blame on the federal government and elicit public sympathy but without any concrete blueprint on how they could be stopped.

Some Pakistani analysts, while flaying these drone attacks, are equally skeptical of the Pakistani stance. Even if e.g. Pakistan acquires or develops drone technology, it is questioned, how will it prevent itself from using against own people, if and when needed in the war against terrorism.[11]

Strategists are of the opinion that the US military has given drones a regular role in 4th Generation Warfare as part of Revolution in Military Affairs (RMAs); hence they will be employed frequently as the US residual forces stationed in Afghanistan after the end of 2014 will become increasingly dependent upon them.

Indian Role in Afghanistan

India is not an immediate neighbor of Afghanistan but sometimes uses the term "extended neighbourhood" to signify its relevance and interest in that country. The memory of five-year Taliban rule in Afghanistan rankles with India when Islamabad-Kabul relations were good and the former had recognised the then Taliban regime. Since the mid-1990s, India pursued anti-Taliban and pro-Northern Alliance (NA) policy.

India is the 5th highest donor in Afghanistan and has invested nearly $2 billion in Afghanistan on many development and reconstruction projects, including highways, dams, and roads and educational projects.[12] It has, in addition, built Delaram-Zaranj Highway to bring Afghanistan-Iran into an economic and strategic alliance. By investing $100 million in building Chahbahar port it has built a road to connect the port to Afghan border, with Delaram-Zaranj Highway.[13] It has invested over $136 million in construction of Ring Road Highway in Helmand province invested over $136 million will connect Chahbahar with Kabul. Work is underway to link Chahbahar by railway line with Hajipak in Afghanistan.[14] The road/rail connectivity will allow landlocked Afghanistan an alternative outlet and thus reduce dependence on Pakistan and other countries.

Like USA and China, India is also seeking access to energy-rich Central Asia and Caspian Sea region and envisions a Chahbahar-Kabul connectivity. It is laying transmission lines and providing Uzbek electricity to Kabul. In addition, hydroelectric Salma Dam, new parliament building and Indira

Gandhi hospital and Habibia College in Kabul are emblems of Indian help. In terms of agriculture and mining it is extending substantial help.

As a manifestation of "soft power," India has implemented more than hundred Afghan-owned small development projects, including free medical care and clinics across the country. Its medical missions in Kabul, Jalalabad, Kandahar, Herat and Mazar-e-Sharif provide free treatment. In the field of education, India provides scholarships to Afghans annually for schooling and training in Indian institutions and teachers and professors in English and other languages. Many of its TV plays, programs and songs are eagerly watched and many Farsi songs reflect Indian tunes.

On October 4, 2011, New Delhi and Kabul signed a Strategic Partnership Agreement (SPA) to bolster their relations. It is involved in training Afghan military and police and other administrative organisations like intelligence agency, RAW, which rejuvenated the KHAD by renaming it RAAM and also helping setting up Central Directorate of Intelligence.[15]

The Indian military is assisting in training Afghan National Army (ANA). The Indian military with the blessing of Iran provided military hardware, repair of Soviet-built Mi-17 and Mi-35 attack helicopters and training facilities to Northern Alliance soldiers to battle the Taliban. The military provided intimate guidance and support to NA forces when they launched attacks in October 2001. Earlier under SPA, India has trained Afghan military and police officers in India and extended some transport helicopters to Afghanistan. The Karzai government has relied on non-Pushtuns to marginalise Afghan Pushtuns and include Tajiks, Hazaras and Uzbeks in most government departments, including the security forces.

President Karzai made his third visit to India in December 2013. He went to India with a "wish list" of heavy weapons and military equipment. India is so far reluctant to honour the request and has only assured training of military and provision of non-lethal supplies. This is due to sensitivities of Pakistan, and apprehensions about getting overly involved in Afghanistan. Besides, most of the heavy weapons are supplied by Russia. President Karzai's motives in seeking military aid from India is to open further options with the US; by making trips he also wants to pressurize Pakistan to force Afghan Taliban to start negotiations with the Afghan High Peace Council (HPC).

As long as Indian military footprint is not present in Afghanistan, Pakistan may not object to the training of Afghan military personnel in India. Afghanistan's vast reserves of iron, copper, cobalt and gold have invited Indian companies to exploit nearly one trillion dollars worth of minerals. This, of course, going to take time and awaits stiff competition from China and others.

India has not confined its activities to Afghanistan but is busy making inroads in Central Asian Republics (CARs) and has made appreciable progress. The Indian military is interacting with Tajikistan security forces and is providing funding for upgrading of air bases and has constructed a military hospital and logistic depot. It inked an agreement in 2007—enabling its air force to establish itself at Ayani airbase near Dushanbe and Farkhor airbase close to northern Afghanistan border. The two airbases have given an option to IAF to strike Pakistan from the rear, if and when needed.

Besides, the Indian Embassy in Kabul India has consulates working in Kandahar, Jalalabad, Mazar-e-Sharif and Herat. Nearly 70 training camps have been allegedly working along Pakistan's western border where Tajiks, Uzbeks, Chechnyans, Arabs and dissidents from FATA and Baluchistan are being funded, trained, equipped and launched into selected regions of Pakistan. The bulk of RAW assets are however deployed in Afghanistan.[16] India's apprehensions in Afghanistan centre around the fact that Taliban, once freed in post-2014 may be launched against Kashmir and Indian military installations like against Indian embassies twice before in 2011. In case they assume total power they will affect Indian access, aid projects, investments, and block access to the Central Asian states as aid and trade corridor. India wants to open its market for export of Afghan goods and wants to integrate Afghanistan into the larger SAARC market.

India officially wants an "Afghan-led" and "Afghan-owned" peace process and a pluralist government but does not want a total control by the Taliban. The same is true of all Afghan neighbors. Pakistan's keenness for "strategic depth" is being diluted now but it still harbors apprehensions of India supporting some Pakistani Taliban and Baloch militants against Pakistan. The Indian army, too, has some benefits and advantages for Afghan forces. Its armed forces are especially trained in counter-insurgencies in Kashmir, northeast and other parts of India and could provide useful training and experience to Afghan forces. However, for any future peacekeeping role in Afghanistan it is not keen—given the bitter experience faced by occupation forces [British, Soviet and the US] on Afghan soil.

India's biggest concern is the post-2014 scenario is that the ANSF is still not equipped and trained enough to confront the Taliban challenge on its own. Heavy scale of desertions, poor pay and discipline structure is evidence of this. Even the police force is not up to the mark and can come under the influence of powerful warlords. India is also unhappy over US-Afghan efforts to induce them to share power. With no appetite to get sucked in the Afghan quagmire it has been inculcating fears in Washington that early withdrawal would open the way for extremist Taliban to regain power and Pakistan to recover its influence in Afghanistan. It has been invoking the possibility of Russia-China, Afghanistan-under-Taliban, Pakistan-Iran-some-Central Asian states bloc coming into being with drastic ramifications for US strategic and economic interests in the region. Likewise, it was hobnobbing with Russia, Iran, Tajikistan, Uzbekistan and Turkmenistan for a possible grouping in case an anti-Indian regime comes to power in Kabul. In case of de facto partition of Afghan state India will back National Alliance, link up with China and Russia and even open channels with Taliban if they control wide areas.[17]

On the suggested options, an Indian seasoned diplomat recommened India to distance itself from the US, support Afghanistan economically and in security matters by training and providing equipment (minus physical presence); remove trust deficit with Iran, CARs and Russia; engage with some elements of Taliban who may be co-opted in future Afghan government; avoid needless criticism of Taliban; and project India in more favorable light than the critical Chinese policies followed in Xinjiang; seek international support for "neutral Afghanistan" to avoid future Chinese influence; and avoid Afghanistan's bifurcation into Pushtun and non-Pushtun areas which are resonant of vivisection of India and threats to peace of South Asia.[18] Further, the proposed energy corridor from Kashgar in China, to Gwadar is viewed with suspicion as it sees China as a competitor. This may be similarly viewed by the US.

Notwithstanding the above, India does not stand eight feet tall in Afghanistan. There is an opinion that Pakistan, as an immediate neighbor, enjoys more advantages and any regime in India—whatever the political coloration—will have to willy-nilly deal with Pakistan. Besides, any Indian or other countries economic assistance in development of Afghan nation will only help Afghanistan stabilise and turn out to be beneficial for regional neighbors. Hence, it is going to be a "win-win" and not a "win-lose" game—unless seen through the cynical lens of real politics. In fact, Pakistan has greater advantages as an immediate neighbor: its relatively big market for aid and trade and technological capacity to assist the Afghan state.

The US draw-down plan has now been modified and it has been decided in principle to leave behind a size-able counter-terrorism force with advisers and trainers till 2014. Since mid-August 2014 Pakistan has launched military operations in North Waziristan with reasonable degree of success after much prevarication.

Pakistan need not compete with India as long as the latter does not have a military footprint in Afghanistan. As far as extending economic aid and help, Pakistan should also do so and thus match Indian influence. "Strategic depth" is now losing its appeal and a developed Afghanistan is considered to be a factor of stability in the region. Moreover, it is up to the Afghans to have relations with any of their neighbors, India or Pakistan but the latter will always be a primary neighbor due to geographical proximity. Pakistan, by skillful diplomacy, needs to retain links with newly-installed government of Ashraf Ghani and Abdullah-Abdullah. Pakistan, too, wants an early exit of US forces but would prefer a residual presence like other regional states till Afghan state stabilises.

A lot depends therefore on stabilisation in Afghanistan and on how Pakistan-India relations unfold in the coming years. According to Michael Krepon, an expert on South Asia, there is good reason to suspect that Afghanistan is too fractious a place for any ambitious state-building. A grand Afghan political settlement is likely to remain ephemeral or illusive. Familiar divides and rivalries will reappear because they have never gone away.[19]

Pakistan's choices are therefore limited. Two generations of Pakistani strategic analysts have held the mirage that Afghanistan provided "strategic depth", where the reverse has proven to be true. Pakistan has been destabilized by its own policies and US misadventures in Afghanistan'; it could be destabilised further if India gains a foothold there as a staging ground to support disaffection in Balochistan. Abida Hussain, a former US ambassador opines that Pakistan is having strained relations with three of its neighbors and hence cannot claim parity with India.[20] Another military analyst darkly predicts that Pakistan-Afghan region has been strife-ridden for centuries: the British, Soviets and Americans tried their military luck and now India is "spreading its wings" by moving towards the Caspian Sea resources through Afghanistan and by weakening the borders. [21]

Conclusion and Some Reflections

A writer has termed post-2014 Afghanistan setting as beset with many earthquakes, political, economic and social.[22] With a society traumatized for over three decades of continued violence, it will take decades to heal the physical and psychological wounds. Overall, international assistance, status and readiness of residual available forces, implication of aid cuts, level and competence of ANSF, the new Afghan government, internal compromise in Afghan society and regional dynamics immediate Afghan neighborhood will be important. And, the recent developments in Iraq-Syria of the Islamic State (IS) in the Middle East could play themselves out ripple through Afghanistan and Pakistan.

Taking a cue from Afghan history, the country for most part has been nominally ruled from Kabul through a strong ancestral tribal warlord system. According to Stephen P. Cohen, Pakistan's future looks like "muddling through" as Taliban may get emboldened against Pakistani government's ambivalent stance and policies and likely Indo-Pak confrontation emanating from intense competition in post-2014 Afghanistan. This was reflected in recent October-November cross-border firing in the west at Line of Control (LoC) and Working Boundary (WB).

Realism suggests that the West may not leave Afghanistan completely after the investment made both in material and human terms in that country. Based on the Soviet experience the West might not allow Afghanistan to fall prey to such a state of affairs that radical elements like Al-Qaeda or Taliban retake control.

No doubt, Western aid and commitment might shrink but their presence will be there in diminished form. Then there is the issue of vast untapped resources of Central Asia close by; China and Russia as competitors are also in the neighbourhood. The rise of China as a regional and potential global power has to be contained: its economic diplomacy is evident in Afghanistan's exploitation of rich untapped sources; nearby Pakistan is unstable and Af-Pak region will remain host to foreign and domestic militants unless Pakistan government decides to take effective steps to enforce its writ in FATA. Moreover, Pakistan is a nuclear weapon state and misgivings, though unwarranted, lurk about their accidental use, or control by militant elements. Besides, Iran is close by and a strong neighbor of Afghanistan. US-relations remain somewhat tense despite easing of recent tensions. The US has built military bases and fortifications in Afghanistan and is expected to remain there for a decade or so. Of course, Afghanistan will have to agree with the US on the issue of signing of Bilateral Security Agreement (BSA). Drone attacks, most probably, will continue and be directed from safe bases with little Western presence on the ground. The new advances in cyber technologies (4th Generation Warfare) will be increasingly utilised in future counter-insurgency wars. While Pakistan continues to protest about the drone strikes but to no avail.[23]

Many politicians use anti-drone rhetoric either to divert blame on the federal government or the US. In fact, according to an analyst, the drones are an issue but not 'the main issue'—at best only a 'side show.'[24] The main issue is how to revive the economy in tribal areas through education, energy development, law and order, exports and trade and generate employment. The dire economy, which if not handled soon, could descend the region into post-2014 bitter conflict.[25] Many politicians use anti-drone rhetoric either to divert blame on the central government or the US to ward off internal pressure. On the Afghanistan scene, the rise of new warlords, opium cultivation and funding may continue and may revert to a pattern where powerful local actors continue to engage with a central government for extracting favors but not offering total loyalty. As always these warlords, when faced with shortage of funds, resort to opium trafficking and illicit trade and depend upon external neighbors for support and help. The Central government will remain weak and unable to exercise control in collecting revenues, conducting trade, maintaining proper legal system and will remain under pressure, should the conflict economy thrive. As a result, newly emerging middle class will suffer the most and opt for emigration abroad or towards bigger cities.

The armed forces, although sizably built over the years, remain generally ill-equipped, ill-trained and ill-armed under pressures desert or break ranks. In other words, Afghanistan for a decade or so shall remain a "rentier state"—relying on a mix of funding sources from inside and abroad. In addition, urban-rural differences will create tensions and inter-generational conflict might take place. A lot therefore depends upon regional powers and international community and their commitment to stabilize. Even if it has the ANSF and raw materials, such as gems, copper, gold and other strategic minerals, time and money are needed to exploit them.

Given Afghan history, peace and reconciliation have been always a problem. The problems are compounded by a plethora of negative factors: scars of war, dangers of reconciliation, warlordism, regional ambitions and weak institutions, poor governance and armed forces, and above all, lack of strategic direction and focus from the US. A writer opines that the greatest tragedy of Afghanistan has been that if it were assisted by international community the situation of the last three decades could have been averted.[26] That this has not happened is testimony to the sins of omissions and commission of Afghan leadership, regional neighbors and generally the international community. With military interventions in Iraq, Libya, Egypt and Yemen, and proxies fighting in Syria the US would be loath to intervene now as robustly as before.

The culturalist historians document the history of Afghans which is based on tradition for *badal* (revenge) and vicious opposition to foreigners and against all invaders and occupiers. A British historian of Indian and Afghan history postulates that the present situation is a replay of old Afghan wars.[27] But culture is not immutable and it changes in tribal societies which have morphed through education, reforms and foreign exposure. Perhaps Afghanistan, a landlocked state, with difficult terrain and lack of centralized nature has prevented this from happening. A writer informally remarked to this scribe while in Kabul that if the British colonial rule had included

Afghanistan (like India, Pakistan and Sri Lanka) in its fold perhaps they would have been different than today.[28]

The overall outlook, therefore, remains fuzzy with a mix of variables in a state of flux—leading to different scenarios. Moreover, presently Washington too does not have any coherent plan which makes the situation more complex. Mr. Shamshad Ahmad predicts the "potential for upheaval" since no clear victor has emerged in Afghanistan e.g., like after Napoleonic wars, World War I and World War II. So in his view, another round of 'Great Game' is in the offing with far-reaching regional implications.[29]

The Pakistani government's November 2014 visit by Afghan President Ashraf Ghani sending waves of IDPs and military action against Taliban elements are welcome steps. The military operation *Zarb e Azab* launched in mid-August against North Waziristan has been partially successful although sending waves of IDPs. But given the Taliban terrorists' acts in Pakistan, destruction of schools and government properties, suicidal attacks on security forces, minorities and innocent people, non-acceptance of Pakistani Constitution and imposing impossible conditions like their own version of *Shariah*, any meaningful negotiations are going to be difficult.[30]

The Afghan Taliban are fighting against foreign occupation but want a united Afghanistan, albeit demanding a greater share under the post-election dispensation. This is not so in case of Pakistani Taliban who are adamant to capture state power and impose their own brand of regressive Islam. At the moment, there is no consensus on whom to talk to and what to talk as the Taliban are splintered into nearly 56 factions.

It is high time the Pakistani government enforce the writ of the state or else what Antonio Gramsci remarked reconcile with the "parcelled sovereignty" of the state. Both Pakistan and Afghanistan have a unique opportunity to turn around the negative developments into a gainful opportunity. In this regard, the international community should contribute towards this effort. Many opine that normalisation and eventual settlement of Kashmir dispute between India and Pakistan could help unlock doors for cooperation in Afghanistan too. The underperforming SAARC region could then open up greater economic activity after the post-2014 US transition.[31]

Pakistan, on its part, has to fortify and seal permeable western borders,[32] put its house in order, forsake "big power" ambitions, avoid treating Afghanistan as a strategic backyard and eliminate domestic militant elements by enforcing the state writ. In addition, it must try to build "soft power" to match India's forays in Afghanistan, promote regional connectivity and attain the goodwill of Afghans and others in the region.

END NOTES

1. On different scenario see Maqsudul Hasan Nuri, "Military Withdrawal: Prospective Scenarios for Afghanistan and the Region" in *International Intervention in Afghanistan: Motives and Approaches,* (Eds.) Arpita Basu Roy *et al* (New Delhi: Shipri Publications, 2002), pp. 61-77.
2. "Afghan refugees can operate accounts, get driving permits," *The Express Tribune* [Islamabad Edition], 18 Aug 2013, p.3.
3. Ibid.
4. Ibid. See "Envisaging Secure and Independent Afghanistan Post-2014: Perspectives and Strategies of Conflict Resolution from the Neigbourhood," Pakistan Policy Group, FES, New Delhi, 2013.
5. See Assunta Nicolini, "Looking beyond the refugee paradigm: the case of Afghanistan," *The Express Tribune,* 16 September 2013, p. 7.
6. See Khalid Koser, "Afghanistan 2014: A Crisis of Internal Displacement," 30 August 2013, GCSP, Geneva, Switzerland.
7. Ibid.
8. On this read, Maqsudul Hasan Nuri, "The murky side of drone technology," *Frontier Post* [Islamabad Edition], 7 January 2014, p.7.
9. Kamal Siddiqi, "Droning on and on," *The Express Tribune,* 24 June, 2013, p.7.
10. John Kerry's statement as cited in "Kerry foresees US troops in Afghanistan after 2014," *The Express Tribune,* 2 August 2013, p.4.
11. See Huma Yusuf, "The drone test," *Dawn,* Islamabad, 22 July 2013, p.6.
12. "Indian interests and perspectives in Afghanistan," *Frontier Post,* 17 January 2014, p.7.
13. Ibid.
14. Ibid.
15. Ibid.
16. Brigadier (retd) Asif H. Raja, "India and Afghanistan," [Opinion Maker], *Frontier Post,* 7 November 2013.
17. See Rupa Kjoti Borah, "India Challenges in Afghanistan Post-2014," South Asia, Masala, NU, Canberra. Australia, 9 August 2013.
18. See Satish Chandra, former deputy national Security advisor, Ministry of External Affairs, Government of India, "Debate on India's Options in Afghanistan," *Strategic Analysis,* IDSA, New Delhi, Vol, 35, No.1, January 2011, pp.125-127.
19. Michael Krepon, "After 9/11," *Dawn,* [Islamabad Edition], 29 September 2013.
20. Syeda Abida Hussain, Former ambassador to the US "The Express Forum: Abida terms talks with India at parity as 'fiction,'" [The Express Forum], *The Express Tribune,* 17 August 2013, p.9.

21. Lt. General (retd) Ghulam Mustafa, former Corps Commander, Mangla Garrison, Ibid.
22. For details see Vanda Felbab-Brown, *Brookings Institution,* Washington D.C., 24 September 2013.
23. See Editorial, "Drones and terror sanctuaries", *The Express Tribune,* 14 September 2013, p. 6
24. Hasan Askari Rizvi, "The search for a new drone policy," *The Express Tribune,* 3 June 2013, p.6.
25. Ibid.
26. Ambassador (retd) Shamshad Ahmed, "Peace or chaos beyond 2014?," *The Express Tribune,* 27 April 2013, p.7.
27. See William Dalrymple, *A Deadly Triangle: Afghanistan, Pakistan and India* [Brookings Essay], Brookings Institution, Washington D.C., 25 June 2013.
28. Based on informal conversation by the author with an Afghan scholar in Kabul (March 2007).
29. Shamshad Ahmad, *op. cit.*
30. See Editorial, "Dialogue blues," *Frontier Post*, Peshawar, 9 February 2014, p.6.
31. Most of the points are derived from presentations by scholars at IDSA-GIGA Bilateral Dialogue on "New Challenges and Partnerships in "The Age of Multipolarity: Indian and European Perspectives" – Session IV, New Delhi, India.
32. On this see Maqsud Nuri, "Border Control and Digital Technologies," *Frontier Post*, 10 December 2013.

8

The Iranian Government and Afghanistan

Bahram Amirahmadian

Hamid Karzai ex-president of Afghanistan had said that after 10 years of presence, activities and operations, the coalition foreign forces were not able to provide security and stability in Afghanistan. Not only Afghanistan, but also world society, mainly neighbouring countries had many challenges with the situation evolving in Afghanistan. Instability, drug trafficking, terrorism, extreme Islamist movement (Taliban and Al Qaeda) and so on, made the situation worsen in Afghanistan that negatively influenced the situation of the region as well as world society.

Struggle and fighting against terrorism did not show positive results. For example fighting against PKK by Turkish government since 1980, still continues, and a lot of money are spent. PKK after arresting its leader faced with some changes in their strategy from a militant and guerrilla movements to a political front, but aftermath, at last came back to the starting point, and the same situation exist. If the money who spent on fighting against PKK could be spent on investing and developing in south and south-eastern parts of Anatoly, it may result in some positive development in the region and could have lessened the clashes.

In Afghanistan, with its unstable situation, we could say that after 10 years of presence of coalition forces, there is still instability and terrorism. Why has the situation not changed in the desired direction? One of the key elements of the continuation of *Talibanism* is that it is supported by domestic residents of rural areas and financed by outside actors. As the President of Afghanistan clarified, the tribal structure of the societies of the border areas, cannot be controlled by the governments of two sides.

Iran has more than 900 KM common border with Afghanistan. From the beginning of Soviet occupation of Afghanistan this border has become the nightmare for Iranian governments. When Afghanistan was occupied by the Soviet army, many of the Afghans contrary to their rich history of fighting against occupiers and invaders, escaped (not migrated) to neighbouring countries. Those who were *Shia* crossed Iranian borders, at the same time they belonged to lower classes of Afghan community, and were poor people, most of them illiterate and non-skilled. Those who were *Sunni* Muslims fled to Pakistan. And those who were technocrats and literate, merchants and businessmen fled to West, mainly Europe.

At the threshold of Iranian revolution the situation in Iran was not stable and the revolutionary council had no governing experiences and plan to govern Iran, faced with the Afghanistan crisis. *Ayatollah Khomaini*, the leader of the revolution in response to fleeing of millions of Afghans to the Iranian eastern border, said that: Oh they are our Muslim brothers and our guests, let them enter our territory. The first prime minister of interim government, *Mehdi Bazergan* said: We expected rain but we faced food. It means that they were not expected that the Shah regime will collapse within a few months. So, from that historical and political point of view Iran was hosting million of Afghani refugees that had damaged Iranian society and population structure. We have a phrase in Persian literature: guest is like fish, after three days it will spoil. Ones may says that the Afghani unskilled human power have a great role in Iranian GDP while they earn less than Iranian manpower. It is true, but they denied many work opportunities from Iranian workers.

There are more than 100 thousand cases of illegal marriage of Afghani men with Iranian women. According to Iranian civil law, marriage of Iranian with foreigners should be register only under formal permission of Iranian government.

Drugs: One of most important issue related to Afghanistan is drugs, whether trafficking or consumption. Every year a lot of smuggling transit drugs from Afghanistan to Europe via Iran, are confiscated by Iranian border police. During three decades of their activities, 3400 Iranian police has lost their lives against drugs trafficking protection.

Afghanistan's Opium Products

For preserving Iranian borders against Afghan smugglers and drugs trafficking, Iran needs a lot of military forces as well as equipments and budget. According to the Iranian news agency, within 8 months of the last year Iranian border police confiscated 343 tonnes of opium production from Afghani smugglers. It has been said that they are able to confiscate only 40 per cent of transit drug trafficking to Europe via Iranian territory.

The rate of crimes among Afghani refugees in many Iranian regions is more than Iranians. There are negative imaginations against Afghanis among Iranian communities. In many regional courts of Iran there are a lot of crimes have been done by Afghani refugees.

The future of Afghanistan after 2014, when international troops withdraw from there for Iranian government could be according to following scenarios:

A. The optimistic case is that Afghanistan military and police force (about 350 thousand) will be able to protect the country and make it stable. Iran will have close relations on economic activity, security, culture, education and development of Afghanistan in a condition that a realistic government comes to power in Afghanistan and has cooperation orientation. Otherwise there will be no changes in the present situation.

B. The American and NATO will stay in Afghanistan according to the military cooperation and keep some military bases in any situation. Iran will not be interested to develop its relations with Afghanistan, because in that case Iran will have to recognize the presence of its traditional enemy (America) in its neighbouring country. (Although in its north-western neighbour in Turkey-Iran is bordering with NATO, but this case is quite different).

C. Withdraw of foreign troops from Afghanistan, the government of

Afghanistan will not be able to provide security for country and Taliban forces come to power. In that case the security of Iranian eastern border will be a case of insecurity and Iran has to settle military forces in the front line and the situation will be very hard and fragile. It is natural that Iran is concerned about its security. Iran's security in east parts of its territory, directly depends on the situation in Afghanistan's central government as well as the situation in east of Iran and west of Afghanistan.

D. There will be no authorized government even Taliban in Afghanistan to govern the country and civil war will cover the country and any local powers try to separate their own territory and some kind of local government come to exist. This scenario, not only for Iran, but perhaps for other neighbours of Afghanistan will be dangerous. Because all neighbouring countries have potentials for disintegration. For example the idea of an independent *Pashtunistan*, Great Baluchistan, *Great Khorassan*, as well as East Turkistan, will make the situation hard and not only regional powers perhaps the powers like India, Russia and China in adjacent region will be concerned about the situation and will try to play a role in terms of their own interest and concerns. This is more pessimistic scenario.

Iran's view on Afghanistan is a realistic one. We are interested that Afghanistan will be able to be independent. And its military and police forces will be able to cover the country and provide its own security. Iran likes to have very close multilateral cooperation with Afghanistan in many fields. Iran considers Afghanistan as a friend and brother country with many common culture and history, with common Persian language and would like to be in a stable situation and share its development in industry, agriculture and cultural issue with Afghanistan. When Afghanistan becomes stable, it is natural that Afghani refugees from Iran will be able to return to their own country and it will improve the economic, cultural and social situation in Iran.

Iran is interested to improve the economic situation in Afghanistan and is able to provide Afghanistan in the fields of education, agricultural sector to replace economic corps instead of opium production. In following pages the economic cooperation between Iran and Afghanistan in the border in terms of insecurity in their common border has been described.

Iran and Afghanistan Economic Cooperation in the Borders Issues

Afghanistan and Iran have 946 KM common borders. There are about 3 million Afghani refugees that they are living in Iran which only 850 thousands of them are registered and 450 thousands have labour visa. The rest are living illegally. The west and north of Afghanistan has Persian culture, all those people who they are living in this part of country, look towards Iran. The Persian speaking population of Afghanistan literary fed by Iranian publication and Persian literature.

Some of Afghani refugees are living in Iran since Afghanistan occupation by Soviet Army in 1979. They have assimilated in Persian culture and Iranian livelihood. They lived and worked in Iran and have got several skills in different fields. Many of Afghani refugees have spent their life-time in Iran. Any arrangement about Afghanistan should not be done without considering Iran's interests and concerns.

It has been reported that around 3 million Iranians citizens (especially youth) have become addicted by narcotic substances which is rooted to Afghanistan. Afghanistan is the main producer of drugs in the world. Iran is neighbouring with this country. According to official reports for protection of drug trafficking from Afghanistan, about 3230 Iranian border police have been killed by Afghani drug smugglers. The areas bordering Iran-Afghanistan are undeveloped areas both sides. Lack of natural resources, including farm lands, water resources, limited precipitation, illiteracy, unskilled manpower, rural population, lack of investment and so on, are the main reasons for underdevelopment.

Afghanistan as a land-locked country needs Iran's territory to have access to free waters. From the beginning of the establishment of Afghanistan, this country benefits from Iranian territory in this regard as well as Pakistani territory. Kabul, the capital city of Afghanistan has been located in Eastern part of country and due to this location has to have closed relations with Pakistan and established roads connections from there to free waters. The distance between Kabul and Islamabad is 370 KM while it is 1619 km. to Tehran. The main problem is that the road connection between Kabul in the east and Herat and *Mazar-i-Sharif* in west and north-west of Afghanistan is not a good road. Although the distance between Kabul to Herat is about

837 km. but it is at the same time dangerous. While there is no good road network in the east-west direction, the authority of central government remains weak. This connecting road (Kabul–Herat, from the central part of country), from mid-1390 is under construction.

Positive Points in the Afghanistan community

Existence of skilled and educated government structure and traditional communities, that promote legitimacy of central government. Establishment of national army and police, preparing of about 375 thousands of military personnel are very important. Many achievements on education are considerable. All those positive development resulted to prepare high level cadres and staff in technological and scientific fields. Political parties and parliamentary activities, NGOs, developed mass media and so on are all hopes for better future.

Economic Cooperation

Iran has played an effective role in the process of restoring peace in Afghanistan by taking an active part in the talks within the 6+2 Group, making considerable efforts in facilitating the Bonn Agreement and supporting the legitimate interim, transitional and permanent Afghan government and providing assistance for the reconstruction of Afghanistan.

Addressing the international Conference on Assistance to Afghanistan's Reconstruction, Dr. Kamal Kharrazi, the Iranian Foreign minister, reaffirmed that: "Iran will allocate US$ 560 million for Afghanistan in the framework of five year assistance plan in the following manner":

1. An annual US$ 50 million as aid. (US$ 250 million in total)
2. An annual US$ 50 million as line of credit. (US$ 250 million in total)
3. An annual US$ 12 million as humanitarian assistance (US$ 60 million in total)

The provision of the above assistance through a five-year plan in indicative of Iran's confidence in the Afghan reconstruction process and its long-term planning to help bring it about. It is noteworthy that Iran ranks first among the donor countries. Iran reiterated its commitment for the period 1383-1385 (2004-2007), at the follow-up conference, held in March 2004 in Berlin, and stated that, in addition to its previous pledge, a further official development assistance amounting to US$ 4 million would be allocated for Afghanistan's reconstruction in 1383 S.H., March 2004 to March 2005. It was further announced that in cases where Iranian companies were selected to carry out the projects, Iran would assume 10 per cent of the cost in each case.[1]

Considering all the issues mentioned above, the two neighbouring countries have no choice but to cooperate in many fields mainly economic and as well as security issues. The main branches of common economic cooperation between two countries in bordering area are: Trade, Transportation, Agriculture, Education, Construction, Mining. Iran has got many experiences in these fields and will be able to teach it to Afghani communities directly, without need of translation.

Natural resources such as Afghanistan minerals in north, petroleum and natural gas, water basin and man power which will be available in very low costs, are the potentials of future development. As we know, two great neighbouring and close countries such as Iran and India has common interests and concerns on Afghanistan.

The future of the region is dependant on solving many problems. In the future the population will be the most important issue. All regional countries are faced with high rate of population growth. In 2050 the population of Afghanistan will increase more rapidly than Iran. By the rate of 2.5 population growth in Afghanistan, it has been estimated that it will increase to 76.3 million. And Iran with the rate of 1.3 will have 100 million population. Uzbekistan, another highly dense populated region country will have 42 million in 2050.

The limitation of natural resources mainly water will be an issue of conflict and disputes. The dispute between Uzbekistan with Tajikistan and Kyrgyzstan on water exists. Afghanistan and Iran will need water that is limited in their territory. Tajikistan has a rich resources of water. By constructing *Raghoun* hydro power station, huge amount of the electricity production will be available to be exported. In the future it is able to export hydroelectric power to the regional countries. Tajikistan itself needs hydrocarbon fuel, which Iran has.

India for its economy will need new resources of energy. And at the same time it will need a big regional market to export goods and service. Afghanistan need foreign direct investment in its rich iron ores mine in its northern areas also extracting, processing and export production of metals, all need road networks. As we know it may say if China is interested to invest in Afghanistan, it will do all by itself. But we should take into accounts that from geopolitical ideas it will be vulnerable if the trade partner are limited.

India should pay attention to Afghanistan's future and has already showed interest to work with Iran in *Chahbahar-Dogaroun-Herat* connecting road networks. Supply and demand of economy could join hands in the region. Iran could supply hydrocarbon energy mainly natural gas. We are working on a long term strategy to meet our needs by neighbours in the region.

A corridor will introduce in the south-east of Iran from *Chah Bahar* port in Oman Sea in the direction of south-north, which meets *Dogharoun-Eslamgha'e-Herat – Mazar-e Sharif – Central Asia*. Iran has allocated 50 hectares in the port area to Afghanistan to establish its own structure for export and import as well as other economic related activities. India is also interested on it.

Here from North will run the electricity transfer line, water pipeline and road and rail to the south direction. And from south to north, goods and services both from India and Iran will transfer in the same points. Afghanistan rich mineral resources will play a key role here. Water, electricity, gas, petroleum, goods and passenger will change the structure of the region. It is necessary to gather and think about the future. Regional countries more than ever need to work together and solve their problem to be ready for future. Today is better than tomorrow. The time is passing fast and we should be fast, otherwise tomorrow will be late.

Afghanistan's trade with Iran in 1392 (Iranian Calendar equal to 21 March 2012 to 21 March 2013) was US$ 2449.7 mil. (including 2417.4 export of Iran to Afghanistan (7.7 per cent of Iran's total export) and US$ 32.3 mil. import of Iran from Afghanistan (about 0.07 per cent of Iran's total import). Iran plays a significant role as a trade partner for Afghanistan.

Checkpoints

There are two customs gate between Iran and Afghanistan. One of them is *Dogharun* in the north and *Milak* in the south of border line. *Dogharoun* (Opposite *Islam Qal'e* city in Afghanistan) is the main customs office between Iran and Afghanistan border and is located in *Dogharoun* city in east of Iran in Khorassan Razavi province. This check point is active all the day. According to official records of Iranian Customs organisation in 2012 about 600 thousand passengers have passed through this gate (about 4 per cent of total Iran) including 259 thousand arrivals and 350 thousands departures. The role of Milak (opposite Zaranj city in Afghanistan) is not considerable and only about 78 thousand passengers (less than 0.2 per cent of total Iran) including 39 thousands arrivals and the same figure departures.

Establishing a Special Economic Zone in *Dogharoun*

Iran has a plan to establish a special economic zone in *Dogharoun*, close to Afghanistan border. This special economic zone spread over 8,000 acres, approved within 250 KM of the border, Mashhad, Islamic Republic of Iran and the Islamic Republic of Afghanistan in *Razavi Khorasan* which is located on the eastern border. *Dogharoun* area is for thousands of years in business. East-West highway, despite the political changes in the world and in different historical periods, has maintained its position and importance. Right now the most important export *Dogharoun* borders Iran and Afghanistan to the land border with the outside world, especially Europe and the Persian Gulf states and is one of the most important transit routes crossing in the world, including international transit corridor north-south corridor TRACECA (Transportation Corridor Europe-Caucasus-Asia) and 16,000 KM of Corridor rail and highway corridor Asian Silk Road. *Dogharoun* special area in the main passageway, in the office, business, warehouse, industrial, residential, academic and service activities will be. With starting this economic zone several job vacancies will appear.

Oil Exporting Pipeline to Afghanistan

According to news (1 October 2012), Iran decided to build an oil exporting pipeline to Afghanistan. Iran will be building a pipeline to export oil to

Afghanistan, Head of the Office of the Campaign against Smuggling Goods and Foreign Currency, *Fada Hossein Maleki* said, Shana reported.

Maleki noted that upon the approval of the Cabinet of Ministers, the pipeline to Afghanistan will be built from Iran's *Dogharoon* city (South Khorassan province) to Afghan city of *Eslam Qaleh* (Herat province). "The construction of such pipeline will reduce possibility of fuel products smuggling, and aside from that, the commission for transition will be much lower," *Maleki* noted. He added that the Iran-Afghanistan pipeline will help to avoid long queues along the border of the two countries.

Maleki did not say how much the pipeline construction would cost, yet added that the pipeline would be of some 1500 meters in length. Currently, there is a special economic zone established in Dogharoon, that stores Iran's fuel tanks and fuel products for exports. The constructed pipeline from Iran to Afghanistan would allow to export products and oil directly from the storages.[2]

Trade

According to official report of Iranian custom organisation, in 1392 (21 March 2012-21 March 2013) total trade volume of Iran-Afghanistan was US$ 2449.7 million which US$ 2417.4 million (7.7 per cent of total Iran's export) was export of Iran to Afghanistan and only US$ 32.3 million Iran's import from Afghanistan (only 0.07 per cent of total Iran's import).

Iran Export to and Import from Afghanistan (2001-2011)

Year	*Import*			*Export*		
	Weight (1000ton)	*Value (1000 US$)*	*Share compare to total Iran (%)*	*Weight (1000ton)*	*Value (1000 US$)*	*Share compare to total Iran (%)*
1380 (2001)	0.866	739	0.00	203.7	51927	1.23
1390 (2011)	17.4	10280	0.016	3115.3	2253063	6.66
1391 (2012)	5.3	2463.4	0.00	2542.4	2901800	8.9
1392 (2013)	24.9	32297.1	0.07	3345.9	2417398.3	7.7

The Share of Trade by Customs

Iran has three customs office in common borders with Afghanistan that the main role of cooperation belongs to Dogharoun (and Islam Ghal'e in opposite side). The two others are Milak and Mahiroud. And also there are three common border markets in small scales that facilitate the local trade between two neighbours (including Milak, Mahiroud, Yazdan).

- Yazdan is an Iranian village in border area which opposite it located Afghan village Kalate Nazarkhan.
- Mahiroud is another Iranian village in border area, but the Afghan village opposite is located in Farah province approximately 60 kilometer far from border.
- Milak is an Iranian border village which is located opposite Zaranj city in Afghanistan.

Iran's Import from Afghanistan and Export to Afghanistan in 1390 (21 March 2011-20 March 2012)

Costumes	*Import*			*Export*		
	Weight (ton)	*Value (1000 US$)*	*Share compare to total Iran (%)*	*Weight (1000 ton)*	*Value (1000 US$)*	*Share compare to total Iran (%)*
Dogharoun	6766.4	4517.4	-	1059.9	419605.4	-
Milak	-	-	-	350.8	53767.7	-
Mahiroud	-		-	120.0	21794	-
Milak border market	80.6	33.1	-	106.0	61165.3	-
Mahiroud border market	34.8	15.8	-	162.3	71213.9	-
Yazdan border market	2119.3	615.1	-	66.6	7570.5	-
Total	9001.0	5181.3	-	1692.9	635117.2	1.87

Transit

Afghanistan has an important role in Iran's foreign transit to/from Afghanistan. In 1390 about 1.6 million tons of goods has been transported from Iran to Afghanistan. This figures shows that 16.7 per cent of all foreign transit goods from Iranian customs have been transported to Afghanistan. In return only 125 thousand tons of goods have been transported from Afghanistan to Iran which consist 1.2 per cent of total transit from target countries.

According to the report of Iranian customs organisation during the Iranian calendar year of 1390 (starting March 21, 2011 to 20 March 2012), 10.6 million tons of goods, were transported via the Iranian transit routes, marking a 11.6 per cent growth in weight increase as compared to the corresponding period last year. Iran's total imports and exports have amounted to 38.4 million tons and 66.4 million tons respectively during the above mentioned period. As such, the 10.7 million tons of goods transported through the Iranian territories, account for 27.9 per cent of the country's total imports and 16.1 per cent of its exports.

According to the figures released by the Islamic Republic of Iran Customs Administration (IRICA)'s Bureau of Statistics and ICT, foodstuff constituted 9.1 per cent of the total volume and 5.67 per cent of the total value of commodities transferred via Iran from March 21 to December 21, 2011, with vehicles making up 2.5 and 8.8 per cent of the total figures in terms of weight and value respectively, fuel accounting for 32.7 and 10.3 per cent, and other goods 55.5 and 75.3 per cent.

Afghanistan has got first rank about transit of vehicles from Iranian territory. In 1390, about 62153 vehicles have been transported to the destination of Afghanistan which constitutes 1/3 of these items and stands among three main countries of transit from Iran. Transit of food items from Iran via Afghanistan in the same period was 335 thousand tons, which constitutes 34.6 per cent of total food items transit from Iran.

Among Iran-Afghanistan borders customs, from Dogharoun customs 19.5 per cent and Milak 11.8 per cent of total food items have been transported to Afghanistan. Among 5 main transit destinations countries from Iran, Afghanistan has got second rank with transiting 1.6 million tons of goods, which constitutes 16.6 per cent of total goods in transit. Protection of illegal border passing, cooperation monitoring, common borders for drug trafficking, promoting trade and safe transit of goods and passengers are other major issues related to the transit.

END NOTES

1. Iran and Afghanistan's Reconstruction, The Headquarter for Afghanistan, Ministry of Foreign Affairs of the Islamic Republic of Iran, December 2004
2. *Trend News Agency*, 1 October 2012, 15:49 (GMT+05:00), Azerbaijan, Baku, Oct. 1 / Trend S.Isayev, T. Jafarov/

REFERENCES

The Islamic Republic of Iran Customs Administration (IRICA) annual reports. http://www.irica.gov.ir/Portal/Home/

World population data sheet, 2011, Population Reference Bureau, www.prb.org

Trend News Agency, 1 October 2012, 15:49 (GMT+05:00), Azerbaijan, Baku, Oct. 1 /Trend S.Isayev, T. Jafarov/

9

Soft Power Diplomacy of Kazakhstan – New Approach Towards Regional Security?

Elnara Bainazarova

Over the past few years, considerable interest in the scenarios of the future development of Afghanistan and regional security, in connection with the forthcoming withdrawal of the ISAF troops is in the spotlight. The forthcoming withdrawal of the troops is pushing Central Asian states to pursue new foreign policy approaches to address the emerging security challenges. Security in Central Asia is challenged by several factors of national development in Afghanistan, which still lacks the social rooting of political and, more general, public institutions, burdened with a weak economy, facing the militarized approach to the human security issues, etc. The issue is becoming even more crucial after the Astana OSCE Summit, where the concept of "Eurasian security" was first declared, APEC Summit in Vladivostok 2012—Putin's idea on flexible involvement of Eurasia to the Asia-Pacific and the US shift to the Asia-Pacific region with the "New Silk Road" programme.

These processes are in the highlight of public discussions in all Central Asian countries. Particularly in Kazakhstan it's the subject of a special attitude. In April 2013 Almaty hosted the III Ministerial Conference of the Istanbul process on Afghanistan. During the meeting President N. Nazarbayev noted that "...the key for solution of Afghanistan issues is in the hands of Afghan people and government as the official representative of the nation. The international community should foster development of the inter-afghan dialogue. Those who demonstrate readiness for establishment of peace and accord in Afghanistan must receive our support. In this regard, the presidential elections scheduled for 2014 in Afghanistan are of paramount importance. We hope, a newly elected head of state will receive support from the whole afghan society."[1]

All above-mentioned trends in regional politics create new security environment for the dynamically developing Kazakhstan, which strives to implement new soft power tools in the region, relying on the Asian regionalism principles. The recent presidential decree "On the Concept of foreign policy of Kazakhstan for 2014-2020" emphasizes more precise the soft power diplomacy strategy of Kazakhstan in the short-term perspective. The concept was developed in accordance with the instructions given in the Address of the President to the Nation "Kazakhstan – 2050 Strategy: New Political Course of the Established State".[2] The concept is a set of essential principles, approaches, goals, priorities and tasks in the sphere of foreign activities of Kazakhstan.[3]

Adoption and implementation of the concept will allow:

- To strengthen national, regional and global security;
- To form favorable external conditions for Kazakhstan, strengthen friendly, equal and mutually beneficial relations with other countries of the world;
- To achieve a higher level of integration of Kazakhstan into the international community and economic relations on the basis of diversification of the national economy;
- To create conditions for economic integration of the countries of the region;
- To intensify international cooperation in the cultural, humanitarian, scientific, educational and other spheres;
- To strengthen legal protection of citizens and legal entities of Kazakhstan, their personal, family and business interests abroad.

Among the key strategic directions of the long-term development of

Kazakhstan are investing in human development, improvement of institutional environment, development of science-drive economy, accelerated formation of infrastructure, strengthening of integration into the global and regional economies. An important innovation was the extension of the concept of "near neighborhood" as one of the first strategic priorities of Kazakhstan foreign policy. Being located in the heart of Central Asia, makes it crucial to maintain close relations with neighboring states. This relates primarily to promote economic and political development, regional stability and security, to counter new soft security challenges and threats.

As a neighboring state, Kazakhstan is interested in sustainable and stable development of Afghanistan and is ready to work with international partners to promote the socio-economic rehabilitation of the country. The recent reforms in foreign policy concept of Kazakhstan strives to implement Asian regionalism features (multilateralism, non-formality, consensus) with a special emphasis on official development assistance program (ODA) for Central Asia and Afghanistan and a special operating agency—KazAID.

Kazakhstani approach is reflected in the approved plans of action for six separate packages of confidence-building measures within the Istanbul Process, which, in turn, represents a significant step towards the implementation mechanism for the peaceful development of Afghanistan. Not excluding the radical development scenarios in terms of enhancing the terrorist threat, drug trafficking, etc., today Kazakhstan presents its vision on reconstruction of Afghanistan. Existing challenges in the domestic politics of Afghanistan as a possible strengthening of inter-ethnic struggle for power and the radicalisation of religious groups can be addressed through social policy, improving the quality of life, investment in infrastructure projects. During the past five years, the government of Kazakhstan has already allocated more than 52 million USD to the recovery program of socially important facilities (schools, hospitals, railway lines), the training of Afghan students, support for agricultural production, participation in the reconstruction and construction of new dams and fortifications, power plants modernisation, etc.

In this regard Kazakhstan advocates an active Afghanistan's involvement in integration processes in region, the strengthening of mutual economic and humanitarian cooperation, including the ways through stirring up of the

Kazakh-Afghan intergovernmental commission's activity, promotion of Kazakhstan's production and investments on the Afghani market, the training of the Afghani qualified experts in Kazakhstan in the fields of economy, industry, finance, transport and education. For example, Governmental Action Plan on assistance to Afghanistan for 2007-2008 has successfully been accomplished. Financial funding has been provided for construction of a variety of civil assets such as school in Samangan province (160,000 USD), hospital in Bamian province (570,000 USD), Kundus-Talukan asphalt road (1,650,000 USD). Overall 2.4 million USD has been transferred to the account of the Afghan Ministry of Finance. Besides, 2,000 tons of milling wheat has been provided as a humanitarian aid to Afghanistan. Up to now Afghanistan has received from Kazakhstan in general about 14,300 tons of food assistance. What is more, the educational program of Kazakhstan for Afghan students allocated 50 million USD. In accordance with this program up to 1000 Afghans are being provided with higher education in Kazakh universities during the period from 2010 to 2020.

In particular, transport and logistics projects are to be strengthened by the Kazakh proposal for granting the Aktau port for freight transport from Afghanistan. Great strategic interest is paid to the project of Trans-Afghan gas pipeline (TAPI), a route which passes through the Turkmenistan-Afghanistan-Pakistan-India, providing an additional influx of Turkmen gas supplies to South Asia. Thus, the economic network in the region will allow engaging the countries of Central and South Asia. These modifications of existing routes may serve as an example of cooperation between Central Asia and all major economic powers on the Eurasian continent.

Full development of the inter-afghan dialogue will be possible only if there is a multilateral cooperation among regional players. Experts in the region have long discussed prospects of involving Afghanistan in transport and logistics network in South and Central Asia, thus providing a basis for trans-regional cooperation in the Eurasian space. By the way, the American concept of the "New Silk Road" also calls for the evolution of the Afghan factor of security threat in the character of mutually beneficial cooperation and economic prospects in the region.

In this regard ODA policy of Kazakhstan should maintain the national interests in order to provide sustainable and prosperous neighborhood and foster bilateral socioeconomic cooperation in the region.[4] More active and focused international development policy of Kazakhstan meets the national interests, as it will contribute: to stabilize the socio-economic and political situation in the partner countries, to prevent illegal migration flows, to fight against terrorism and extremism, to maintain "secure neighborhood belt", to strengthen the international position and positive image of Kazakhstan.

Nevertheless, until recently, Kazakhstan's participation in development assistance on a bilateral basis, for objective reasons, was very limited in scope, geography and forms of aid. Kazakhstan's development aid experience on a multilateral basis is much wider in scope, which was conducted under the UN auspices, through voluntary contributions and participation in the trust funds, including projects in the field of environment, population, health, women's rights, aid for landlocked countries, fight against drug trafficking, etc. In 2011, this cooperation has exceeded 2 million USD. In 2012, the amount of voluntary disbursements of the Republic of Kazakhstan to international organisations, which can be defined as development assistance, comprised more than 418 million KZT.

What is more, according to the UN statistics, during 2006-July 2011 Kazakhstan's allocated 53.7 million USD as a humanitarian foreign aid, the main part of which was distributed to Central Asia. With the indicator of 30 million USD Kazakhstan ranks the third in terms of humanitarian aid volume in the region.

In general, Kazakhstan's allocated about 100 million USD as humanitarian aid and ODA both. However, the absence of a systematic approach in this field results in low efficiency and poor project management, which don't give the ground for desirable political and image outcomes for the country.

Kazakhstan's ODA policy will seek the following purposes:

1) assisting in tackling the global and regional sustainable development issues, including the problems of poverty, international crime, drug trafficking and illegal migration;
2) assisting in socially oriented economy building;
3) developing political, economic, educational, social, cultural and academic relations with foreign countries;

4) maintaining the good neighborhood area within the Kazakhstan borders;
5) developing trade-economic cooperation with partner countries and stimulating integration of capital, goods, services and labour markets;
6) strengthening the authority and promoting the positive perception of the Republic of Kazakhstan in the international community.

For the planned period of 2014-2016 Central Asia and Afghanistan are to be the main recipients of Kazakhstani ODA. Fulfilling the main principles of the ODA Concept for maintaining good neighborhood policy and poverty alleviation in the region, the ODA program could mainly focus on "CA+Afghanistan" format.

The comparative analysis of the HDI development shows, that the current socio-economic development indicators have a specific impact for Kazakhstan. Compared to other CA states, achievements of Astana are highly important in the overall regional development dynamics, gaining extra points for country's positive image and investment attractiveness, ranking as a high human development country (UNDP statistical data). But at the same time a growing development rating gap between CA states pushes for negative influence to Kazakhstan through the increasing pressure on its' labour market, the real risks to the security of its borders, and on the national business investments in the economy of these countries.

Afghanistan has advanced the combination of modern constitutionalism with the traditions of a tribal society. The creation of the High Peace Council is one indicator for this, but the ongoing accommodation between old and new is also visible in the daily life of urban Afghanistan: traditions prevail, but the search for a cautious accommodation of modern ways is also present. Afghanistan has reached certain progress in terms of education (girl attendance of schools and universities); social services (health care) and infrastructure, including water and energy supply. Afghanistan has established a new security model, where the Afghan National Security Force (ANSF) with roughly 400,000 troops (260,000 Afghan National Army (ANA) and 160,000 Afghan National Police (ANP). Afghanistan has consolidated the security situation in the Northern part of the country, especially in Balkh province, and in the Kabul area.

Comparative table of the Kazakhstan ODA Programme Priority Region Countries (2012)

Country	*GNI per capita, USD*	*HDI rank*	*HDI*	*Life expectancy at birth (years)*	*Satisfaction with quality of education (%)*	*Employ-ment of population ratio (%)*	*Poverty index High human development*
Kazakhstan	10,451	69	0,754	67,4	49,9	75,0	0,002
Medium human development							
Turkmenistan	7,782	102	0,698	65,2	74,3	62,6	-
Uzbekistan	3,201	114	0,654	68,6	85,0	62,8	0,008
Kyrgyzstan	2,009	125	0,622	68	46,7	70,4	0,019
Tajikistan	2,119	125	0,622	67,8	76,4	70,3	0,068
Low human develop-ment Afghanistan	1,000	175	0,374	49,1	58,5	53,8	-

Source: Economic and Social Survey of Asia and the Pacific, 2013, Human Development Report, UNDP: 2013.

Despite this, the HDI development remains too low and the following issues still needs to be tackled:

- Afghanistan lacks the social rooting of political and, more general, public institutions.
- Afghanistan is constrained by a weak judiciary and by institutions that can exist on their own without the huge financial contribution of the donor community;
- Afghanistan is burdened with a weak economy, 70% of which are still based on drug production. The promise of future explorations of raw materials does not generate new revenues for the state within the next five to ten years, at best;
- Afghanistan is confronted with a huge demographic challenge that translates into the urgent need for millions of new and sustained jobs;
- Afghanistan is still facing the militarized approach to the human security issues;
- The excessive donor-dependency of Afghan institutions has rather supported the rent-seeking-structures in the Afghan social fabric. It has also generated an overly strong bureaucratisation in order to

coordinate and integrate external policy approaches with Afghan national objectives.

It's worth noting the key principles of Kazakhstan's ODA policy as the following:

- focus on horizontal cooperation models, when the donor-recipient relations are conducted on equal "win-win" basis;
- priority of technical assistance to transfer complex know-how and experience in a number of areas in which Kazakhstan has a high level of competence;
- transparency of decision-making upon the aid allocation;
- accountability of the national budget funds allocated to ODA;
- coordination of measures taken by Kazakhstan in the field of ODA with other bilateral and multilateral donors;
- decreasing the number of overlapping ODA programs;
- consideration of ecological and social impacts of the relevant projects and measures of ODA;
- expression of growing interest by the recipient country in the progressive development of the bilateral cooperation with Kazakhstan;
- the use of an individual approach with a comprehensive account of the political, economic, social and national characteristics of each recipient state.

Operating budget of the ODA TA Grant policy is expected to comprise 0.01% of the GDP for the initial period of 2014-2016, 15 million USD, consequently, the sum would comprise approximately 22.5 million USD and 30 million USD in the following years.

The amount of operating budget for the initial period (15-22 million USD) limits the multidimensional aid types, including tied credits and service-fee-based loans. For the 2014-2016 all aid disbursements are envisaged to be allocated in a tied aid grant form, including both direct bilateral aid and multilateral channels through co-financing with international aid agencies. The next period of 2017-2020 might be based on the concessional functionality of ODA, increasing the loan share of ODA up to 60%.

Period	*Grant share of total ODA, %*	*Loan share of total ODA, %*
2014-2016	50	50
2017-2020	40	60

Loan share includes debt relief and tied credits.

Shares of Total ODA, %

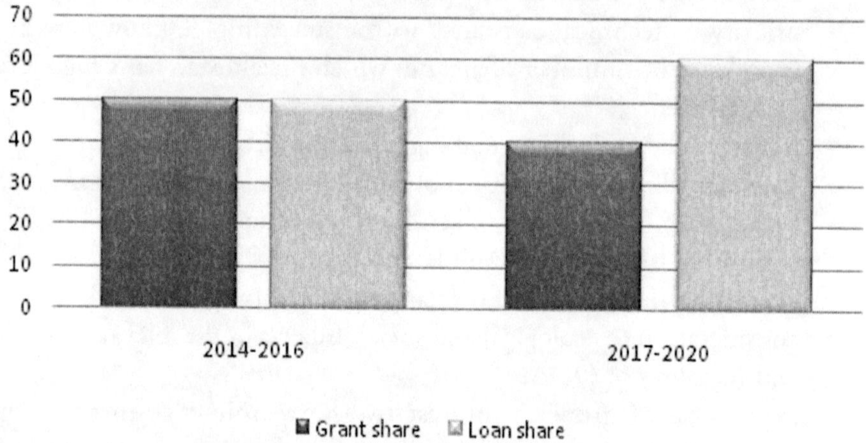

Channels and Forms of Assistance

Channels	*Share of total aid, %*
Bilateral (Humanitarian aid, technical assistance, administrative costs)	50
Multilateral (via IDB, ADB, etc.)	50

As per international experience of other aid agencies the Kazakhstani ODA could be divided in two main types (on non-return (**grants**) and on return (**loans**) basis) where ODA of first type is managed/coordinated by KazAID and classified as follows:

(1) **Technical Assistance (TA) Grants (project-wise)**

1.1. Project consultancy (preparation of FS, tender docs, project supervision)

1.2. Professional training (seminars, on-job training, re-qualification, advisory service)

1.3. Capacity building (local centers of competence, office equipment)

1.4. Support of direct NGOs activities in concerned countries
1.5. Joint international projects (with other donors)

(2) **Technical Cooperation (TC) (program-wise)**
2.1. Education of non-residents in Kazakh universities/centers in required fields of competence
2.2. Exchange of knowledge/experience with counterparties/partners

(3) **Humanitarian Aid**
3.1. Supply of emergency assistance (medical help, pharmaceuticals, basic food, desinfection) (upon Ministry of Emergency Situations)
3.2. Sustainable recovery (engineering and education services, basic health treatment, training, construction)

In particular, Kazakhstani aid has to avoid the common mistakes of the previous donor aid experience of other countries, when the local mentality and local needs issues were ignored and the inefficient programs for good governance or public administration, democracy building were imposed. Hence, Kazakhstani aid aims to tackle the most important needs of the recipient countries, focusing on social and economic infrastructure and services.

Aid Distribution by Sectors

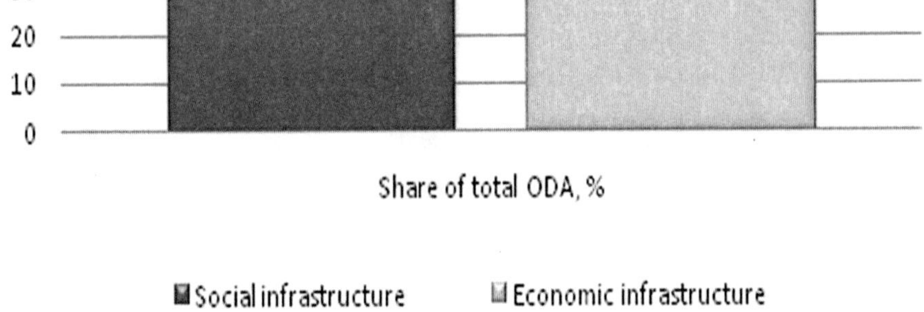

Aid Distribution by Sectors for the Initial Period (2014-2016)

Sectors	*Share of total aid, %*
Social infrastructure	60
Primary education	
Health care	
Water and energy supply	
Cultural	
Sanitation	
Economic infrastructure	40
Transport and communications	
Agriculture and integrated rural development	
SME support (incl. microfinancing)	
Tourism and mutual trade	
Total	100
Extra expenditures:	-
Debt relief	-
Emergency aid	-
Administrative costs	-

A gradual transition from the interpretation of ODA as a tool of "soft" power into the "smart" power will be the main goal of Kazakhstan's foreign policy in the long-term perspective. Thus, Kazakhstan's foreign policy should enter into the context of deep intellectualisation of international politics. Complementing the economic power with greater investments in "soft" power, we can create a framework for answering tough global and regional security challenges.

END NOTES

1. President addressed Ministerial Conference of Istanbul Process for Afghanistan. Central Communications Service // http://ortcom.kz/en/news/president-addressed-ministerial-conference-of-istanbul-process-for-afghanistan.1223
2. Address by the President of the Republic of Kazakhstan, Leader of the Nation, N. Nazarbayev "Strategy Kazakhstan-2050": new political course of the established state", 14 December 2012 // http://www.akorda.kz/en/page/page_poslanie-prezidenta-respubliki-kazakhstan-lidera-natsii-nursultana-nazarbaeva-narodu-kazakhstana-
3. Concept of the Foreign Policy of the Republic of Kazakhstan for 2014-2020, 30 January 2014 //http://www.akorda.kz/ru/page/page_215843_o-kontseptsii-vneshnei-politiki-respubliki-kazakhstan-na-2014-%E2%80%93-2020-gody
4. Presidential Decree "On Official Development Assistance Concept of the Republic of Kazakhstan", 9 April 2013 // http://online.zakon.kz/Document/?doc_id=31374898

10

Afghan Factor in the Regional Security of Central Asia

Ildar Yakubov

Introduction

The general decrease of international presence and attention to Afghanistan determines a new situation in and around the country. Experts and analysts identify a growing role of new factors in the political development of Afghanistan, such as a crucial place of political system of the country and the "regionalisation" of the Afghan problem. Afghanistan is a traditional source of security threats for Central Asia. The prospects of Afghanistan after 2014 can be considered in the context of the probability of changing security threats and the balance of power in the region. At the same time it is obvious, that regional security threats in Central Asia, emanating from Afghanistan is felt most clearly in neighboring countries. Uzbekistan is a leading actor among them. Its position and relations with Afghanistan play an important role in ensuring the regional security and promoting efforts to stabilize the situation in the IRA.

Afghanistan: Trends and Prospects

Many observers consider events of 2014 as a milestone for the future of Afghanistan. Conclusion of the withdrawal of ISAF and the presidential elections were indicated as key factors of internal dynamics. But if official, Kabul and the international forces could achieve real military successes and a political settlement with the opposition. In this context it is important to recall that the strategic decision for a phased withdrawal of ISAF was the result of clear understanding about the impossibility of military solution to the Afghan conflict. The lack of military solution means that the opposition is also unable to come to power by force. Fragmentation of the opposition forces has become a reality. It seems that the Taliban movement was united only by having a common external enemy. Now the Taliban has gradually transformed from the earlier monolithic structure, which ruled Afghanistan in the 1990s.[1] From the other side, the proponents of Kabul, primarily among ethnic minorities, also seek to ensure greater freedom of action, guided by their own interests and goals. Besides, in the recent past, the Najibullah regime held "Kabulistan" without a military presence of the Soviet army. Crucial event for his regime was not the presence of foreign troops, but the termination of external aid. As a result, the influence of the withdrawal of international forces has less impact than expected on intra-Afghan balance of power. The real question becomes the volume of international assistance for Kabul.

Unsuccessful attempts of a political settlement reinforce the military stalemate in Afghanistan. The negotiation process took place in an atmosphere of a complete mutual distrust and unclear conditions for compromise. The main difficulty lay in the definition of the real intentions of the parties. Meanwhile, the process of negotiation found at least three independent parties to the conflict—the U.S. and Kabul entered into separate and secret talks with the opposition often independently. The opposition also represented two groups—the Taliban and the "Hezb-e Islami" of Gulbuddin Hekmatyar. As a result, a search for compromise and political settlement was reduced to the "talks about talks". The refusal of the Taliban to participate in the presidential elections has reinforced the feeling of failure.

Obviously, in this context the presidential elections lose a significant portion of its capacity for reconciliation and, consequently, undermined the legitimacy of the political transition process. Meanwhile, Washington as a key external "player" in Afghanistan demonstrates the lack of a political strategy in the final stage of its Afghan campaign. The U.S. was not able to reach an agreement on the participation of all parties in the presidential elections. Washington is not involved in dealing with the situation in Afghanistan, but more interested in "saving face" and ensuring the secure withdrawal.

The unclear and confusing situation in Afghanistan gives space to analysts to predict "post-2014" transformations.[2] Among the worst-case scenarios is "chaos" in Afghanistan or the restoration of the rule of the Taliban. Both of them include a new phase of civil war. The continuation of current trends is the most likely to be the scenario and has similar consequences. The best-case scenario is a phased successful reconciliation and reunification of the country under the new president of Afghanistan. Though Frederic Grare argues, "building best- and worst-case scenarios is a relatively futile exercise",[3] it is important to note in the context of this subject, that any of scenarios does not expect even the possibility of a direct military attack on a Central Asian state.

Threats to the Central Asia Regional Security in the Context of Afghan Problem

The key factors—the withdrawal of ISAF, uncertainty about the progress in Afghanistan, vagueness about the possible political agreement between the government and the opposition—raise the level of threats and challenges to the regional security in Central Asia. First of all, it is likely to expect the intensification of activities by terrorist and extremist forces connected with Afghan groups. It is an obvious and impending challenge. These groups may enjoy covert support of some foreign powers, interested in destabilizing the situation in some countries of the region and based on their own tactical goals. The most vulnerable to instability may seem Tajikistan and Kyrgyzstan. Both counties have serious internal risks and potential sources of instability, and extremely limited resources to counter these threats and protect their borders from infiltration. Subversive activities of terrorist and extremist forces from the territories of Tajikistan and Kyrgyzstan against neighboring states in the region cannot be excluded. In this case the north of Afghanistan has a strategic importance.

Another problem is the risk of refugees fleeing from Afghanistan. A large number of Afghan Uzbeks, Turkmen and especially Tajiks may flee to Central

Asia in the case of "chaos" in Northern provinces of Afghanistan. Waves of refugees could lead to serious humanitarian crises; there is a possibility of conflicts between population of Central Asian countries and Afghan refugees; a large number of refugees could undermine the fragile economies of poorest countries, such as Tajikistan.[4] Drug trafficking is one of the most dangerous types of non-traditional security threats in Central Asia. The region is the most convenient corridor for transportation in Russia and further Europe. Now Afghanistan produces about 75% of world opium production.[5] Probably, drug trafficking will become more systematic; its structural and resource bases more organised and would assume a secure character after 2014.

The unpredictability of the situation in Afghanistan creates apprehensions about mindless supply to and arming the Afghan National Security Forces (ANSF) with modern weapons and military equipment. It can disrupt the balance of military power in the region and may contribute to the unchecked proliferation of arms in the long term. A full or partial collapse of the ANSF will lead to the militarisation of Central Asia. Planned reduction of the Afghan army is just a little bit better scenario, because "ex-servicemen will have to search for new sources of income".[6]

Another kind of threat is a new round of geopolitical competition in Central Asia. It is likely that Washington will establish its permanent military bases in Afghanistan. Russia is already seeking to expand and strengthen its military and political foot hold in the region. It is likely to intensify efforts to involve countries of the region in Russia's geopolitical orbit. Moscow may manipulate the "Afghan threat" to achieve its goals. The withdrawal of ISAF and the lack of a political settlement in Afghanistan are not conducive to realise the potential of economic development of Central Asia. Further escalation of Afghan conflict would entail the deterioration of economic development in the region, restriction in energy supply, communications, trade and economic relations, finally stalemating and freezing of the planned projects in Afghanistan. It is likely that investment attractiveness of Central Asia will decline, and it will have a negative impact on the socio-economic situation and sustainable development of the region. If the best-case scenario will be implemented, another sort of problem can emerge. Successful development of agricultural sector of the north of Afghanistan will mean emergence of a new "player" of the sharp water conflict in Central Asia.

Afghan Factor and Opportunity of Cooperation for Uzbekistan

Central Asia feels that Afghanistan is strategically important. Operations in Afghanistan are an important part forming a geopolitical role of the region. Conclusion of the withdrawal of ISAF from Afghanistan means the end of the Northern Distribution Network and the declining political, economic and military attention to Central Asia. Features of the new situation are a reduction of U.S. influence and simultaneous rise of China and partly Russia. Possible competition between India and Pakistan in Afghanistan will also affect Central Asia. U-turn in relations between Iran and the West could lead to emergence of a new powerful actor in the region.

Meanwhile, there are growing apprehensions that Central Asian countries may alone face the Afghan problem. Obviously, the neighboring countries of the region are able to provide less impact on the events in Afghanistan compared to others—Iran, China or Pakistan. But a relatively active position of neighboring states of Central Asia is determined by a large number of Afghan Tajiks, Uzbeks and Turkmen and forming trade and economic dependence of northern Afghanistan. Uzbekistan is the most influential Central Asian country in relation to Afghanistan. It has relatively significant resources that could contribute to the international community for reconstruction, economic assistance and ensuring the long-term stability in Afghanistan.

They include:

- developed transport and communications infrastructure, which is an important "bridge", linking Afghanistan with the outside world;
- large Uzbek diaspora in Afghanistan, numbering about 3 million people;
- level of relations between Uzbekistan and leading powers involved in the Afghan conflict.

Uzbekistan's position on Afghanistan is based on the principles, set out in the Concept of Foreign Policy of the Republic of Uzbekistan, adopted in 2012.[7] According to it, Uzbekistan "does not participate in military-political blocs, and reserves a right to leave any interstate formation in case of its transformation into a military-political bloc". Also it "shall not allow deployment of foreign military bases and facilities on its own territory".[8]

Republic of Uzbekistan "pursues good-neighborly and friendly policy towards Afghanistan, remaining committed to the principle position of non-interference into the internal affairs of the country, building relations with it on a bilateral basis, assisting and supporting a government that will be elected by the Afghan people".[9] It is interesting to note, that Uzbekistan supports "formation of an interim government, which could include the main forces of this country".[10] It is likely that Uzbekistan seek to exclude any possibility of the involvement in the intra-Afghan conflict and any "geopolitical game" in and around Afghanistan. Simultaneously Tashkent will take measures to activate the international dialogue on a political settlement in Afghanistan. For this purpose Uzbekistan may try to establish and promote open communications with different Afghan forces and key actors in and around Afghanistan, and also with the regional and global "players".

Conclusion

The current dynamics of internal development are due to the complex processes associated with the state of permanent strategic uncertainty in the country. The presence of the ISAF in Afghanistan could not negate the impact and the role of the militant groups and organisations in the military and political scheme of things in Afghanistan. The situation is further aggravated by the lack of strategy of the U.S. and its allies in Afghanistan. It has a vital importance to seek a good-neighborly and friendly policy both for Central Asian countries and Afghanistan. The uncertainty of "post-2014" scenarios suggests an intensification of trade and economic cooperation with Afghanistan to establish political stability in the country and accelerate the implementation of joint projects for their completion.

One of the major projects in this area is the construction of the railway Hayraton-Mazar-Andhoi, connecting Uzbekistan and Afghanistan. It is an important contribution to the peace process. Implementation of such projects demonstrates an ability to generate and realise ideas of non-military efforts to stabilize the situation in Afghanistan. Such efforts appear to be the most promising in the current context of the Islamic Republic of Afghanistan. Uzbekistan has to actualize the need for rapid response to security threats and challenges emanating from Afghanistan. It gives the opportunity to minimize the inevitable damage of the growing tensions in regional security, and improve resilience to external risks.

END NOTES

1. See: Kenneth Katzman, *"Afghanistan: Post-Taliban Governance, Security, and U.S. Policy"*, Congressional Research Service, January 17, 2014, pp.13-17. www.fas.org/sgp/crs/row/RL30588.pdf
2. See, for example: Xenia Dormandy and Michael Keating, *"The United States and Afghanistan: A Diminishing Transactional Relationship"*, January 2014, http://www.chathamhouse.org/sites/default/files/public/Research/Asia/0114DormandyKeating.pdf; Michael O'Hanlon, *"The intelligence assessment is too pessimistic about Afghanistan"*, January 3, 2014, http://www.washingtonpost.com/opinions/us-intelligence-is-too-pessimistic-about-afghanistan/2014/01/02/eacde5a6-719b-11e3-9389-09ef9944065e_story.html; etc.
3. Frederic Grare, *"Afghanistan Post-2014: Scenarios and Consequences"*, February 2014, p.7, http://www.gmfus.org/wp-content/blogs.dir/1/files_mf/1391544902Grare_AfghanistanPost2014_Feb14.pdf
4. Jos Boonstra, Marlène Laruelle, Sébastien Peyrouse, *"The Impact of the 2014 ISAF Forces' Withdrawal from Afghanistan on the Central Asian Region"*, January 2014, p.19, http://www.eucentralasia.eu/fileadmin/user_upload/PDF/other_related_publications/EC-Study-Impact-of-the-ISAF-Withdrawal-on-Central-Asia.pdf
5. Ian S. Livingston and Michael O'Hanlon, *"Afghanistan Index"*, Brookings Institution, January 10, 2014, p.18, http://www.brookings.edu/~/media/Programs/foreign%20policy/afghanistan%20index/index20140110.pdf
6. See: Jos Boonstra, Marlène Laruelle, Sébastien Peyrouse, *"The Impact of the 2014 ISAF Forces' Withdrawal from Afghanistan on the Central Asian Region"*, January 2014, p.18, http://www.eucentralasia.eu/fileadmin/user_upload/PDF/other_related_publications/EC-Study-Impact-of-the-ISAF-Withdrawal-on-Central-Asia.pdf
7. *"Uzbekistan to adopt Concept of Foreign Policy Activities"*, July 2012, http://www.uzdaily.com/articles-id-19556.htm
8. *"Foreign policy"*, Ministry of Foreign Affairs of Uzbekistan, http://www.mfa.uz/en/cooperation/policy/?sphrase_id=2311
9. *"International cooperation"*, Ministry of Foreign Affairs of Uzbekistan, http://www.mfa.uz/en/cooperation/
10. *"International cooperation"*, Ministry of Foreign Affairs of Uzbekistan, http://www.mfa.uz/en/cooperation/

11

Afghanistan after the US Withdrawal: A Look from Kyrgyzstan

Y. Emre Gürbüz

Introduction

US-led NATO operation in Afghanistan opened a new phase in the strategic game between the US and Russia, since the US obtained a stronghold in Russia's "near abroad", in Kyrgyzstan. The Unites States has evacuated its air base in Kyrgyzstan, and this will radically change the situation in Afghanistan after 2014.

The American physical presence in Central Asia was authorised by Russia and regional powers' consent, as the expansion of extremism in Afghanistan was to the disadvantage of all regional states. The thread of extremism and the US-led operation of coalition forces in Afghanistan created unexpected—open or covert—alliances between Russia, China, Iran, India, Central Asian Republics and the US.

The operation is conducted by NATO with 49 troop contributing states named as International Security Assistance Force (ISAF). The coalition forces include most of European countries, and it consists of a long list of countries from El Salvador to Togo. The main contributor is the US. As of June 2013, 68,000 of the total 97,920 troops are from the US.[1] In June 2011, 101,000 of the total 140,000 troops were American soldiers. Indeed the operation was led by the US, and their withdrawal is followed by other members of ISAF. France, Canada and Australia had already left Afghanistan; second biggest contributor, Great Britain with 8,000 soldiers, will also leave by the end of 2014.[2]

After the substantial withdrawal of the US troops even wider, deeper, more constructed and lasting alliances are required in the formation of an Afghan-led solution to the complex situation in Afghanistan. Regional states were not among the contributors of ISAF. The closest ally to Afghanistan was Azerbaijan. After the withdrawal, regional powers are expected to take more active role in Afghanistan. A shift might occur replacing the US-led ISAF operation to an Afghan-led operation with the support of regional states.

Because the key air base of the US troops operating in Afghanistan was stationed in the capital of Kyrgyzstan, Bishkek, this article will first give some information about the air base, and then it will focus on the implications of the US withdrawal from Central Asia with a look from Kyrgyzstan.

Manas Air Base in Bishkek

The air base was opened in December 2001, right after the 9/11 attacks. It was one of the two US military air bases used during the "Operation Enduring Freedom" launched against Taliban, which held power in Afghanistan, since 1996. The other US military air base was in Karshi-Khanabad, Uzbekistan. Following the "May 2005 Unrest" in Andijan, Uzbekistan, US-Uzbek relations are strained and the US had to withdraw its forces from the Karshi-Khanabad Air Base in November 2005.[3] Since then, Manas Air Base is the only US military air base operative in the war in Afghanistan outside of Afghanistan itself. Kyrgyzstan is also the only country in the world with US and Russian military bases, and it will remain so until July 2014.

The mission of the air base is defined as fourfold: "air refuelling, airlift, onward movement of forces and humanitarian assistance and developing partnerships for the long term".[4] Refuelling of planes during flight (air-refuelling) is a significant mission for the operation with long-ranged flights both on the way to and from Afghanistan and for planes operating on Afghan airfield. Equipment and troops deployed from other bases in the west to

Afghanistan were all transferred through Manas Air Base, which was unofficially called "gateway to hell" by the troops. The humanitarian assistance, which was defined among the four missions, is the weakest of realised goals.

There are 1,200 troops stationed in the air base with an additional 900 international contractor personnel. 700 of the contractors are Kyrgyz;[5] others are from a variety of countries with specialists from Western countries and interpreters from Afghanistan. The air base transits yearly 50,000 troops to Afghanistan.

On July 11, 2014, the military air base was closed on the insistence of the Kyrgyz government. The closure of the air base came to agenda in 2006, after the election of the Kyrgyz President Bakiyev. Actually, when Bakiyev came to power after the "Tulip Revolution" (2005) by ousting the former President Akayev, it was thought that Bakiyev was supported by the US, and this was a successful move on the "grand chessboard".

Tulip Revolution occurred at a critical period, when colour revolutions of Georgia (2003) and Ukraine (2004)—with American support—were shaking Russia's sphere of influence. Similar to other "colour revolutions", also before the Tulip Revolution of Kyrgyzstan, civil society leaders were trained by experts from the US, the Ukraine and Georgia to promote democracy, opposition newspapers were printed by US sponsored Freedom House, and during the "revolution" NGO's played a leading role. One of the first declarations of the new President Bakiyev was, however, to increase the lease or to close the American air base. Indeed, Russia and China were critical towards the presence of a military air base in Central Asia, and in June 2005, after the US tension with Uzbekistan, Shanghai Cooperation Organisation (SCO) demanded a timeline from the US to evacuate their air bases. The closure of the air base in Uzbekistan was carried out, but the US extended the use of the Manas Air Base by increasing the payment for the air base and related activities. In 2009, President Bakiyev once again pressed for the closure of the air base, but again the rent was increased yearly from $17 million to $60 million, and the lease was extended for another five years. Additionally, the name of the air base was changed to "Manas Transit Center", which did not bring changes to the actual function of the air base, and it is still generally called "Manas Air Base".

After another popular uprising in 2010, President Bakiyev was toppled, and a new government came to power. When the incumbent President Atambayev was elected in 2011, he promised that the lease of the transit centre (air base) will not be extended for another term.[6] Most people, both the citizens of Kyrgyzstan and international observers, thought that this was just another bluff to increase the rent, but Atambayev was resolute in closing the transit centre on the deadline of the final lease, July 11, 2014.

In 2013, Atambayev's determination to close the transit centre was under discussion among the Kyrgyzstani politicians and with the US officials; in June 2013, the closure was approved by the Kyrgyz parliament.[7] Finally, on October 17, 2013, the US announced that they will carry out the transfer of the transit centre to an air base in Romania, Mihail Kogalniceanu Air Base, on the Black Sea. The distance of the new air base to Kabul is three times longer than the Manas Transit Center, and the air-refuelling is not accepted by the Romanian government, which will be carried out by a yet undefined air base in southwest Asia. Mihail Kogalniceanu Air Base was previously used by the US during its Iraq operation in 2003, and it was listed among the "black sites", where infamous interrogations of suspected terrorists were executed.[8]

The Manas Air Base was economically very beneficial to Kyrgyzstan. In addition to the yearly payment for the lease, there are many extra costs, such as the service fees (ca. $21 million), contributions to aero-navigation (ca. $30 million), military local spending (ca. $ 1.5 million) and most significantly jet fuel payments (ca. $99 million) in 2013.[9] This presented a very significant income for Kyrgyzstan. The lease was directly paid to the state, and because of Kyrgyzstan's weak taxation resources, this was crucial for state revenues. Therefore, President Atambayev's declaration on the closure of the air base was not taken seriously until recently. Most Americans in Bishkek still complain about the "insanity" of Kyrgyz insistence, and they underline "their economic contributions to Kyrgyzstan".[10] It is even argued that Kyrgyzstan is not in a position to pay employees by the end of the year without air base's revenues.

The Position of Russia and Central Asian Republics

The increasing number of financial agreements with Russia shows that Russia will cover economic losses of Kyrgyzstan. Russia aims to consolidate its influence in Central Asia, and since 2001, it considered the US presence as a threat. In September 2013, Russia forgave Kyrgyzstan $500 million debt in exchange for extending the lease of its air base in Kant, until 2032, and they promised $1.1 billion worth defence arms. This is directly related to the withdrawal of American troops, but before that in the beginning of 2013, when Kyrgyz new strategic development plan ("National Sustainable Development Strategy for the Kyrgyz Republic for the Period of 2013-2017"[11]) was announced, it was clear that more than half of the projects for the development of Kyrgyzstan would be financially supported by Russia.

Russia also strengthened its presence in Tajikistan. After Kyrgyzstan, Russia also extended the lease of its air base in Tajikistan in October 2013, until 2042. In addition to it, Russia is also taking the control of the Ayni Air Base near the Tajik capital Dushanbe. India invested $70 million between 2002 and 2010 to use the Ayni Air Base, but now the air base will station 7.000 Russian troops.[12] India will continue to use another air base, Farkhor, in Tajikistan.

Russia defined its priorities as fight against terror and drug trafficking. Russia is consolidating the border of Afghanistan with its move in Tajikistan. The mountainous terrain on the border of Afghanistan and Tajikistan makes the protection of borders a very difficult task. The same mountainous terrain continues through the porous border between Tajikistan and Kyrgyzstan, which creates an easy access for terrorists to move from Afghanistan to Kyrgyzstan and then to Uzbekistan or to Sinkiang Uighur Autonomous Region of China. The long border between Kyrgyzstan and Kazakhstan cannot be well protected as well. These borders can easily be passed by drug-smugglers reaching Russia and then Europe. Indeed, this is the most active drug-trafficking route stretching to Europe.

Russia was concerned on the US role in Central Asia. US policy on Central Asia was mainly based on Brzezinski's ideas on Eurasian geostrategy declared in his book "The Grand Chessboard" (1998), where he argued that Eurasia cannot remain under the domination of one power. Central Asia should be an open sphere of influence.[13] Russia, on the other hand, claims that the US is trying to build a unipolar world, while calling for multipolarity in Central Asia, which is the "near abroad" of Russia. Russia supports the formation of a bipolar or multipolar world, which requires restricting the US influence in Russia's "near abroad". Russia's insistence on the withdrawal of the US troops from Kyrgyzstan was based upon these strategic theses. While realistically Russia benefitted from the US operation in Afghanistan and even opened space for American presence, Russia was against the long-term presence of the US in Central Asia.[14]

Apart from these strategic evaluations, the war on terror in Afghanistan was for the benefit of Russia. Afghanistan was functioning as a magnet pulling Islamic extremists from Central Asia and Russia to be isolated or even destroyed in Afghanistan. For example, since the beginning of the "Operation Enduring Freedom", the leading cadres of the Islamic Movement of Uzbekistan (IMU) moved to Afghanistan, joined Taliban and later Al-Qaida to learn armed fighting. They were stating that they would go back to the Fergana Valley to launch an attack on the Uzbek government. When Afghanistan was under Taliban control, IMU tried to enter Uzbekistan trough Batken region of Kyrgyzstan between Tajikistan and Uzbekistan. The first attempt was made in 1999, and it was repeated in 2000. Both attempts confronted by armed resistance of the Kyrgyz army, and IMU had to retreat. Later, American operations forced them to move from North Afghanistan on the border of Tajikistan to Afghan-Pakistan border. In the following years the leading cadres of IMU were killed, while they were fighting on the side of Taliban or al-Qaeda.

After the ethnic clashes in South Kyrgyzstan of 2010, some Uzbeks left Kyrgyzstan to join Islamic extremist movements, and later comeback for avenge. Until now, it is estimated that they are busy with fighting in Afghanistan.

The Position of the US

The US was for a long time physically detached from Central Asia. 9/11 attack and the US operation to Afghanistan opened the doors of Central Asia for the US presence. The US targets were controlling energy sources of Central

Asia; restricting Russia's influence in the region; and fighting the "war on terror".[15] Only the final one was the declared and legitimate objective of the US. This objective was accepted by other countries, such as Russia, China, Pakistan, Iran and Central Asian Republics, as the US was the only power to undertake the costly and dangerous military mission. This gave the US the opportunity to have a foothold in Central Asia's energy resources.

An undeclared but clear objective was that the US aimed to control the energy sources to maintain its position as a world power. It is often recited that whoever controls energy, controls the world; US goal to control hydrocarbon energy sources in Central Asia and West Asia was a direct result of this formulation. Although the US was talking on opening Central Asia to a multitude of international actors, it operated against Russia's interests as it was seen in the example of creating alternative pipelines to Russia, such as the Baku-Tbilisi-Ceyhan Pipeline connecting Azerbaijani oil and gas to Turkish port on the Mediterranean. This pipeline was later aimed to be connected to Turkmen and Kazakh oil and gas pipelines as well. This would end Russian monopoly on the transportation of Azerbaijani and Central Asian hydrocarbon sources, and also weaken Russia's political influence.

Restricting Russia's influence in its "near abroad", especially on the energy rich countries, was considered as the undeclared US target. Russia wanted the US to announce that it will really leave Central Asia after the declared and legitimate target of its presence is achieved. Toppling the Taliban government in Afghanistan was indeed achieved within a month after the US operation was initiated in October 2001. Another target, punishment of the Al-Qaeda leader Osama bin Laden, was achieved by killing him in an operation in May 2011. A month later, President Obama announced the withdrawal of troops. It was followed by a process of transferring the security control to Afghan forces in the summer of 2011 in Bamiyan. On June 18, 2013, last districts on the eastern border and Kandahar were transferred to Afghan Armed Forces.[16] The withdrawal will be completed by the end of 2014, after fighting the last battles against Taliban and Al-Qaeda, and leaving the ground to Afghan forces. The role of foreign troops was expected to be restricted by training Afghan forces. In June 2013, Afghan Armed Force was 185,000 soldiers strong, which is replacing 100,000 soldiers of ISAF.[17] There is also a trained Afghan police (Afghan National Police) with 157,000 personnel.[18]

After long insistence of the Russian and Chinese governments, and additionally Afghan government's decision not to extend the bilateral agreement with the US,[19] ISAF is leaving Afghanistan. Considering the strategic chess game between the US and Russia, now, Kremlin has got the victory but the question is what to do with it!

Afghanistan's Need for Multivector Policies after Withdrawal

The withdrawal of the US will change the power game in Afghanistan. There is a potential of win-win in the cooperation of different countries in Afghanistan. The power struggle in the Greater Central Asia is generally evaluated within the zero-sum-game discourse of the "New Great Game" between the US and the United Kingdom with other NATO allies on the one side and Russia and China on the other side. Actually Russia and the US are the main players and others have minor significance. China is not a direct ally of Russia. It is considered as the balancing power by some Central Asian leaders; China's priority is expanding only economically in Central Asia and Afghanistan for the time being. China constructs transport infrastructure to export its commodities and pipelines to import oil and gas necessary for further economic growth.

The New Great Game is very clearly witnessed in Kyrgyzstan, and the limits of the American and Russian power is also seen obviously. Kyrgyzstan is considered by great powers as a relatively stable and small country, which is financially easy to deal. However, when the ethnic clashes in South Kyrgyzstan started in June 2010, none of these international actors were in a position to intervene and stop fighting sides. In spite of the invitation of the Kyrgyz President Roza Otunbayeva, and despite the fact that this was a golden opportunity for any actor to increase its influence, no step was taken. The calculated disadvantages were more than the advantages. Interference would inevitably trigger firing arms, which would create enmity towards the intervener.

After the events in South Kyrgyzstan, beginning with the second half of 2010, it was witnessed, how a multivector foreign policy came into effect in

Kyrgyzstan. Many countries, including China, Turkey, South Korea, Japan etc., took a much more active role in Kyrgyzstan, incomparable to their previous position. This change was of course made possible by Russia and US, because it was more feasible and realistic to build the stability in Kyrgyzstan by a multitude of international actors. This policy was also welcomed by Kyrgyzstan, because it would give them more flexibility and more autonomy.[20] Cooperation of different countries created a win-win situation.

The bulk of problems in Afghanistan are far more complex than in Kyrgyzstan. Even before the Soviet occupation, Afghanistan was a poor country on its way to modernisation. The search for modernisation, however, found resistance in rural areas from communities with traditional beliefs. The efforts of King Amanullah in 1920s collapsed because of traditional resistance it triggered. During the Cold War, Afghanistan again sought to make reforms for modernisation. A balanced foreign policy between the US and the USSR helped Afghanistan to invest in dams, irrigation, electricity infrastructure and education.[21]

However, the radical social change attempt of the communist PDPA in 1978 was confronted again with a similar opposition. Afghanistan slipped from a balanced policy between superpowers to the battleground of superpowers, following the Soviet intervention in 1979, and the American support for Islamic extremists. After the end of the Cold War, Afghanistan became again the battleground of the new American doctrine on the global threat; this time it was against Islamic extremism. Since late 1970s, wars and civil disorder devastated the country increasing the toll and vitality of the problem to be solved.

Today, the infrastructure for development, the investment in mines, hydrocarbon resources, agriculture and education are not better than they were 35 years ago. Afghanistan also lacks a functioning government with an institutionalized, well-structured and clean political apparatus and a bureaucracy reaching the rural areas. Afghanistan strongly needs financial sources and a functioning state apparatus, for investing in infrastructure and production, but they have neither capital nor income to invest. The solution will come through Afghan-led attempts, but the complexity of the problem requires the support a multitude of international actors.

The priority is in the central government's need of military support, which was sustained by the US. Even under the US support, the Afghan government was not in a position to implement a sustainable development plan. US presence was not able to solve the problems, but it could only contain them for some time. The retreat of the US will create a power vacuum in Afghanistan, and the situation will most probably get worse.

The Possible Results of a Triumph of Extremism in Afghanistan

It is highly expectable that decentralisation of power will continue bringing instability to Afghanistan, which will lead to the growth of extremism. The most significant problem, which can spiral to the whole region, is terror. It can very easily turn to a safe haven for terrorists, which was the pretext of the US intervention and the support for the US intervention by all governments in the region, including Iran, Russia and China.

A possible seizure of the Afghan government by extremists will most probably result in continuous attempts to expand. Not only because of Jihadist goals on creating a Caliphate in Central Asia but also because Afghanistan has limited resources, and it is very hard for any state to survive on minimal resources and with no access to the world.

The first regions to be affected by a regime change in Afghanistan will be Central Asia and Pakistan. In Central Asia the success of extremism seems to be less possible in the immediate future. Extremism seems to have reached its peak point in Central Asian republics for now. If extremism will grow in Central Asia, extremist groups will probably remain localized in the Fergana Valley, until a radical shift occurs.

Even if extremism cannot triumph in Central Asia under given conditions, the terrorist acts will definitely give great harm to Central Asian republics. In the last decade, the extremists had weak influence in Central Asia, and they were rather moving to Afghanistan and recently to Syria to join the war. Illegal border crossings from Tajikistan were rarely reported, but two recent events on Chinese borders indicate another potential of threat. In January 2014, 11 Uighurs from China were killed in Kyrgyzstan near the border after clashes.[22] It was announced that they were Islamic Uighur separatists in search for arms.

It is estimated that Uighur separatists will continue their search for arms. Afghanistan and Uighur region are not far away and mountainous terrain will help mujahedeen to ally with Uighur separatists.

Kyrgyzstan, Tajikistan and Uzbekistan are increasing security measures to confront the threat spilling over from Afghanistan. Uzbekistan revised its laws, and President Karimov "warned citizens who have left the country to join Islamic extremist groups and train at terrorist camps that if they return home they will go to prison". The threat is real. Uzbek mujahedeen have turned to experienced fighters in Afghanistan, and they are known as experts of making explosives in Afghanistan. There is increasing activity being reported in North Afghanistan, and the number of Uzbek mujahideen in war-torn areas is not low. In January 2014, 33 Uzbeks died in a single air strike of Pakistani forces in Pakistani tribal areas.[23]

Kyrgyzstan also announced its concern that "border conflicts have increased. There are external challenges and threats: terrorism, extremism, drug trafficking. But the main challenge for Kyrgyzstan today is the Afghan factor." As a precaution the borders are jointly patrolled with Uzbekistan and Tajikistan.[24] Additionally, Kyrgyzstan and Uzbekistan constructed new border posts.[25] Even if the return of the mujahedeen will not bring a regime change in Central Asian republics, it will still create some harm.

Pakistan seems to be closer to be deeply affected by changes in Afghanistan. Dr. Hasan Askari Rizvi from Pakistan states that "the tide of militancy that kept Afghanistan on the boil all these years is now flowing in reverse, into Pakistan. A resurgence of Taliban in Afghanistan would accentuate this situation, and could create grave problems here for both the government and the military."[26]

Taliban was supported by Pakistan, but Taliban is only one of the political groups in Pakistan among other Islamist and political groups. The rise of Jihadist groups to power in Afghanistan will alter the power struggle in Pakistan, which will have much stronger effects in the region also spreading to India. Afghanistan has limited potential to harm other countries, but Pakistan is a powder keg—not only regionally but also globally with its diaspora.

Another problem is drug-trafficking, which is the only source of income for many Afghans. Hypothetically, growth of opium can be eradicated immediately in areas under government control by employing modern technology, but its immediate extermination will only create more problems impossible to be solved. The solution of this problem only by force will create more poverty, instability and extremism, unless alternative sources of income will be created for the people of Afghanistan. So far, wheat and cotton growth is being supported, but cotton is no match for the cheaper Pakistani cotton and they are never as profitable as opium.

Putting an end to opium cultivation is not only a consequence of international anti-drug policies, but it is also for the benefit of creating a stable government in Kabul and beyond. Drug-trafficking feeds bribery and corruption within the state, and it also increases the power of local groups by creating a source of revenue and a clientelist relationship outside of the state control. Drug-trafficking is not only a source behind the decentralisation of the state, but it also feeds the extremist propaganda against corruption. To put it briefly: Illegal money increases corruption, which leads to a non-functioning state apparatus, injustice and decentralisation, which in turn support the breeding ground of extremism. The drug-trafficking is also one of the fundamental sources of bribery and corruption in Central Asian republics. Corruption and drug use is again one of the main anti-propaganda themes of Islamists in Central Asia.

Possible Solution

The complex situation in Afghanistan can be turned to an opportunity for creating wider cooperation between regional countries. The failure in Afghanistan is to the disadvantage of all states in the region: The secular Central Asian republics' stability will be shaken by terrorist attacks of extremists. China's problem with separatists will be further enhanced. Russia will try to fight extremism in Tajikistan and Kyrgyzstan and will be affected more by terrorist actions in its cities. Iran will be involved by the rise of anti-Shia extremism and Sunni Balochs, who are related to Baloch in Pakistan, might also be influenced by separatist ideas. The power struggle in Pakistan will shift in favour of the extremists, which will also affect India. The dangers thread all, and the solution can only be achieved by participation of all states in the region.

As mentioned above, in Kyrgyzstan the severity of problems softened the power struggle of great powers opening space to third countries. The problems in Afghanistan are more complex, and they require a wider and deeper cooperation. Realistically only a multitude of international actors can handle the severe problems Afghanistan faces, and it is an obligation for all countries in the region to cooperate. The best scenario would be the creation of stronger cooperation in Asia in order to solve this complex problem.

Regional cooperation will not only minimize the threat but it will help to the realisation of the New Silk Road for regional economic connectivity and intraregional trade with roads, media and internet,[27] cultural and scientific exchange, and network for the transportation of goods, oil, gas and electricity. The New Silk Road is proposed by the former US Minister of Foreign Affairs Hillary Clinton for a solution to the Afghan problem, and it lost its appeal with the US withdrawal. A possible election of Mrs. Clinton as the new US President in 2016 can revive this policy, but the problem requires immediate solutions and neither US support nor her comeback are on the table for now. The project should be revived by all related countries.

Another project proposed to create economic revenues for Afghanistan and to establish regional cooperation is Turkmenistan-Afghanistan-Pakistan-India (TAPI) pipeline project. Similar to Baku-Tbilisi-Ceyhan pipeline project is also against Russia's monopoly on oil and gas. When the stability of Afghanistan was achieved under the strong rule of Taliban, US signed agreements to implement TAPI, but Osama bin Laden led attacks to American targets and Taliban support for bin Laden ended this deal. Today this project is still far from being implemented. If the continuing enmity between Pakistan and India makes this project hard to realise, the security question in Afghanistan makes it impossible to find financial support.

The construction of a transit road connecting Central Asia to Pakistan and India through Afghanistan and putting Afghanistan also on the east-west route by the revival of the Silk Road also faces same problems with TAPI. Additionally geographical obstacles of the mountainous terrain increase the economic costs of this project.

Another project about turning Afghanistan to a transit country is the CASA-1000 (Central Asia, South Asia) project, which will supply Pakistan with Kyrgyz and Tajik electricity through Afghanistan. It is expected to increase Kyrgyz and Tajik revenues by power export and to end electricity shortages in Pakistan.[28] The project is promising, but it is confronted by the same problems as TAPI and the New Silk Road.

The main problem is how Afghan security and stability can be achieved? Militarily neither Collective Security Treaty Organisation (CSTO) of Russia, Kazakhstan, Kyrgyzstan, Tajikistan, Belarus and Armenia, nor Shanghai Cooperation Organisation (SCO) of Russia, China, Kazakhstan, Kyrgyzstan, Tajikistan and Uzbekistan are in a position to replace ISAF, NATO (or US) yet. They need to be strengthened by accepting more countries and increasing coordination. Indian Foreign Secretary Sujatha Singh's acknowledgement during the SCO Heads of Government meeting in Tashkent on November 29, 2013, that "India would like to see all countries under SCO umbrella vanquish terrorism from their territories"[29] is encouraging. This was not only a call for the member states (SCO) but also for states with observer status, i.e. India, Pakistan, Iran, Afghanistan and Mongolia.

Afghanistan's national military is being trained and maintained by some countries, which needs to be preserved for an Afghan-led security take over. Although foreign assistance is obligatory, it is worth to emphasize that the new period should be Afghan-led, because US presence has increased enmity towards foreign soldiers, and foreign intervention will create suspicion and confront some resistance.

Military assistance is obligatory but it is not enough. It is clear that Afghanistan's economy should be improved, which can be achieved by constructing of transportation infrastructure connecting Central Asia and South Asia. The rich and unexploited mines of Afghanistan are another crucial source of revenues, which are vital for the reconstruction of a stable government in Afghanistan. Win-win strategies should be constructed with all possible participating countries joining the process in 2014.

However, deeply rooted tensions between the Asian states hinder the implementation of joint international projects. The problem between India and Pakistan is far form being solved. China is in SCO with Russia and

Central Asian republics, their long lasting border dispute with India is being solved recently; they have good relations and mutual economic agreements with the US, but still China is considered as a strong rival and a threat by all of them. Although common concerns might bring them together, it is more possible that competition will create new alliances. Unexpected alliances can occur between the US, Russia, China, India, Turkey, Pakistan, Saudi Arabia, Qatar and Central Asian Republics.

It is clear that the cooperation is for the benefit of all countries in the region and it is sine qua non for success. Although it is hard to expect a wide regional cooperation, it is also true that only severe problems, such as natural catastrophes, can create necessary conditions to change hostile foreign policies and help forming new foreign policies. Afghanistan is a man-made catastrophe, and it has to be solved by widest possible international cooperation. Despite the fact that it seems very hard to establish wide alliances against the common threat, the danger of the worst scenario can become the leverage to make it happen. This is indeed an obligation for all regional actors.

END NOTES

1. International Security Assistance Force, "International Security Assistance Force (ISAF): Key Facts and Figures", June 24, 2013, retrieved from http://www.isaf.nato.int/images/stories/File/Placemats/20130624_130624-mb-isaf-placemat.pdf.
2. "Q&A: Foreign Forces in Afghanistan", *BBC*, June 18, 2013, retrieved from http://www.bbc.co.uk/news/world-south-asia-11371138.
3. "US Plane Leaves Uzbek Base", *BBC*, November 21, 2005; retrieved from http://news.bbc.co.uk/2/hi/asia-pacific/4457844.stm.
4. "Bi-Monthly Newsletter", *Transit Center at Manas* retrieved from http://www.transitcenteratmanas.com/us/important-documents/134.html.
5. Matt Millham, "Kyrgyzstan Bill likely to End US Use of Air Base at Manas", *Stars and Stripes*, June 20, 2013; retrieved from http://www.stripes.com/news/kyrgyzstan-bill-likely-to-end-us-use-of-air-base-at-manas-1.226777.
6. "Manas Contract will not be Renewed in 2014, Kyrgyz Premier Says", *Central Asia Newswire*, August 15, 2011; retrieved from http://www.universalnewswires.com/centralasia/viewstory.aspx?id=4642.
7. "Manas: Kyrgyzstan Backs Closure of US Airbase", *BBC*, June 20, 2013; retrieved from http://www.bbc.co.uk/news/world-asia-22988967.
8. Chris Carroll, October 18, 2013, "DOD to Shift Air Trainsit from Manas to Romania", *Stars and Stripes*, retrieved from http://www.stripes.com/news/dod-to-shift-air-transit-from-manas-to-romania-1.247953.
9. "TCM Financial Contributions", Transit Center at Manas, March 31, 2013; retirieved from http://www.transitcenteratmanas.com/images/stories/tcm_econ_impact_march_2013_eng.pdf.

10. The author of this article lives since 2010 in Bishkek Kyrgyzstan. Information used in this article without citation is based on the author's observations and communications.
11. *Strategiya Ustoichibogo razvitiya Kyrgyzkoi Respubliki na period 2013-2017 gody*, (January 21, 2013).
12. "Russian Army Base Deal with Tajikistan Key to Regional Security - Lawmaker", *Ria Novosti*, Octer 7, 2013; retrieved from http://en.ria.ru/military_news/20131007/183983310.html.
13. Zbigniew, Brzezinski, *The Grand Chessboard: American Primacy and its Geostrategic Imperatives*, New York: Basic Books, 1998.
14. Sergei Markenov, "Avoiding Zero-Sum Game in Central Asia", *Russia Direct*, June 16, 2014, Retrieved from http://www.russia-direct.org/content/avoiding-zero-sum-game-central-asia.
15. S.V. Kulkarani, "India's Engagement with Central Asia: Exploring Future Directions", *Annual International Studies Convention 2013*: 7; retrieved from http://aisc-india.in/AISC2013_web/papers/papers_final/paper_137.pdf.
16. "Q&A: Foreign Forces in Afghanistan", *BBC*, June 18, 2013, retrieved from http://www.bbc.co.uk/news/world-south-asia-11371138.
17. "Q&A: Foreign Forces in Afghanistan".
18. Mirvais Khan and Amir Shah, "Another Female Police Officer Shot in AFganistan", *Yahoo News*, September 15, 2013, retrieved from http://news.yahoo.com/another-female-police-officer-shot-afghanistan-062545180.html.
19. Noorullah Shirzada, "How Many US Troops are still in Afghanistan", *CBS News*, January 9, 2014, retrieved from http://www.cbsnews.com/news/how-many-us-troops-are-still-in-afghanistan.
20. Y. Emre Gürbüz, "Kyrgyzstan: in Search for Stability", *Insight Turkey*, Fall 2013: 191-205.
21. For alternative views of Afghanistan before 1979 see Elizabeth Bumiller, "Remembering Afghanistan's Golden Age", *New York Times*, October 17, 2009, retrieved from http://www.nytimes.com/2009/10/18/weekinreview/18bumiller.html?_r=0; and Mohammad Qayoumi, *Foreign Policy*, May 27, 2010, retrieved from http://www.foreignpolicy.com/articles/2010/05/27/once_upon_a_time_in_afghanistan.
22. "Criminals near the Kyrgyz- Chinese border were Uighur separatists", *Kabar*, January 24, 2014, retrieved from http://kabar.kg/eng/law-and-order/full/8970.
23. Zamira Eshenova, "Karimov Prepares for Terrorists", *Radio Free Europe*, January 24, 2014, retrieved from http://www.rferl.org/content/uzbekistan-imu-terrorism/25241539.html.
24. Shavkat Turgayev, "Raiymberdi Duishenbiyev: The main challenge for Kyrgyzstan at the state border today is the Afghan factor", *24.kg News Agency*, September 23, 2014, retrieved from http://eng.24.kg/cis/2013/09/23/28056.html.
25. Kaliya Duishebayeva, "Five frontier posts to be constructed on Kyrgyzstan-Uzbekistan border", *24.kg News Agency*, June 19, 2013, retrieved from http://eng.24.kg/community/2013/06/19/27334.html.
26. M. Ilyas Khan, "Why Pakistan Fears Foreign Pullout from Afghanistan", *BBC*, retrieved from http://www.bbc.co.uk/news/world-asia-25034112.
27. Stephen Kaufman, "'New Silk Road' Vision Offers Afghanistan a Brighter Future", *Iipdigital*, United States of America Embassy, October 28, 2013, retrieved from http://iipdigital.usembassy.gov/st/english/article/2013/10/20131028285286.html#axzz2r XGYhKvG.
28. *CASA-1000* official Website on http://www.casa-1000.org/index.php.
29. "India Pitches for Greater Role in Afghanistan", *IRNA*, November 30, 2013, retrieved from http://www.irna.ir/en/News/80927957/Politic/India_pitches_for_greater_role_of_SCO_in_Afghanistan.

REFERENCES

"Bi-Monthly Newsletter", *Transit Center at Manas* retrieved from http://www.transitcenteratmanas.com/us/important-documents/134.html.

"Criminals near the Kyrgyz-Chinese border were Uighur separatists", *Kabar*, January 24, 2014, retrieved from http://kabar.kg/eng/law-and-order/full/8970.

"India Pitches for Greater Role in Afghanistan", *IRNA*, Novermber 30, 2013, retrieved from http://www.irna.ir/en/News/80927957/Politic/India_pitches_for_greater_role_of_SCO_in_Afghanistan.

"Manas Contract will not be Renewed in 2014, Kyrgyz Premier Says", *Central Asia Newswire*, August 15, 2011; retrieved from http://www.universalnewswires.com/centralasia/viewstory.aspx?id=4642.

"Manas: Kyrgyzstan Backs Closure of US Airbase", *BBC*, June 20, 2013; retrieved from http://www.bbc.co.uk/news/world-asia-22988967.

"Russian Army Base Deal with Tajilkistan Key to Regional Security - Lawmaker", *Ria Novosti*, Octer 7, 2013; retrieved from http://en.ria.ru/military_news/20131007/183983310.html.

"TCM Financial Contributions", Transit Center at Manas, March 31, 2013; retirieved from http://www.transitcenteratmanas.com/images/stories/tcm_econ_impact_march_2013_eng.pdf.

"US Plane Leaves Uzbek Base", *BBC*, November 21, 2005; retrieved from http://news.bbc.co.uk/2/hi/asia-pacific/4457844.stm

Brzezinski, Zbigniew, *The Grand Chessboard: American Primacy and its Geostrategic Imperatives*, New York: Basic Books, 1998.

Bumiller, Elizabeth, "Remembering Afghanistan's Golden Age", *New York Times*, October 17, 2009, retrieved from http://www.nytimes.com/2009/10/18/weekinreview/18bumiller.html?_r=0.

Carroll, Chris, October 18, 2013, "DOD to Shift Air Trainsit from Manas to Romania", *Stars and Stripes*, retrieved from http://www.stripes.com/news/dod-to-shift-air-transit-from-manas-to-romania-1.247953.

CASA-1000 official Website on http://www.casa-1000.org/index.php.

Kaliya Duishebayeva, "Five frontier posts to be constructed on Kyrgyzstan-Uzbekistan border", *24.kg News Agency*, June 19, 2013, retrieved from http://eng.24.kg/community/2013/06/19/27334.html.

Eshenova, Zamira, "Karimov Prepares for Terrorists", *Radio Free Europe*, January 24, 2014, retrieved from http://www.rferl.org/content/uzbekistan-imu-terrorism/25241539.html.

Gürbüz, Y. Emre, "Kyrgyzstan: in Search for Stability", *Insight Turkey*, Fall 2013: 191-205.

International Security Assistance Force, "International Security Assistance Force (ISAF): Key Facts and Figures", June 24, 2013, retrieved from http://www.isaf.nato.int/images/stories/File/Placemats/20130624_130624-mb-isaf-placemat.pdf.

Kaufman, Stephen, "'New Silk Road' Vision Offers Afghanistan a Brighter Future", *Iipdigital*, United States of America Embassy, October 28, 2013, retrieved from http://iipdigital.usembassy.gov/st/english/article/2013/10/20131028285286.html# axzz2rXGYhKvG.

Khan, M. Ilyas, "Why Pakistan Fears Foreign Pullout from Afghanistan", *BBC*, retrieved from http://www.bbc.co.uk/news/world-asia-25034112.

Khan, Mirvais and Amir Shah, "Another Female Police Officer Shot in AFganistan", *Yahoo News*, September 15, 2013, retrieved from http://news.yahoo.com/another-female-police-officer-shot-afghanistan-062545180.html.

Kulkarani, S.V., "India's Engagement with Central Asia: Exploring Future Directions", *Annual International Studies Convention 2013*: 7; retrieved from http://aisc-india.in/AISC2013_web/papers/papers_final/paper_137.pdf.

Markenov, Sergei, "Avoiding Zero-Sum Game in Central Asia", *Russia Direct*, June 16, 2014, Retrieved from http://www.russia-direct.org/content/avoiding-zero-sum-game-central-asia.

Millham, Matt, "Kyrgyzstan Bill likely to End US Use of Air Base at Manas", *Stars and Stripes*, June 20, 2013; retrieved from http://www.stripes.com/news/kyrgyzstan-bill-likely-to-end-us-use-of-air-base-at-manas-1.226777.

"Q&A: Foreign Forces in Afghanistan", *BBC*, June 18, 2013, retrieved from http://www.bbc.co.uk/news/world-south-asia-11371138.

Qayoumi, Mohammad, *Foreign Policy*, May 27, 2010, retrieved from http://www.foreignpolicy.com/articles/2010/05/27/once_upon_a_time_in_afghanistan.

Shirzada, Noorullah, "How Many US Troops are still in Afghanistan", *CBS News*, January 9, 2014, retrieved from http://www.cbsnews.com/news/how-many-us-troops-are-still-in-afghanistan.

Strategiya Ustoichibogo razvitiya Kyrgyzkoi Respubliki na period 2013-2017 gody, (January 21, 2013).

Turgayev, Shavkat, "Raiymberdi Duishenbiyev: The main challenge for Kyrgyzstan at the state border today is the Afghan factor", *24.kg News Agency*, September 23, 2014, retrieved from http://eng.24.kg/cis/2013/09/23/28056.html

India and Afghanistan

12

India's Afghanistan Policy post-2014 in need of Geopolitical Constructivism

Ambrish Dhaka and Ahmadullah Archiwal

Geopolitics of Afghanistan

Afghanistan's geopolitics has been historically nuanced in innumerable ways, but the contemporary essence of all lies in being a state-space without adequate institutionalisation of international order of states. This being simply that Afghanistan lacks a stable agency that can communicate with international institutionalisation of states within its territory. This refers to state's contribution to international security, economy and globalisation as putative culture. The post-9/11 development has tried to salvage the situation with a push to constitutional democracy and justice system that brings Afghan state into transpiring range of law and norm that constitute sovereignty in the international order. The year 2014 marks a watershed in due course as for the first time the elections would be conducted for Presidential and Provincial councils largely under the apparatus of the Afghan state-agencies albeit externally aided by ISAF and international donors. These elections would test the credibility of state to withstand the rebellious force in the wake of imminent drawdown later in its aftermath. One of the important facets to understand is that the connotation of Af-Pak looms large on future state-stabilisation, which is going to remain for a while under purview of relationship that Afghanistan shares with Pakistan. The cross-border rebellious forces are potent enough to weaken the democratic process in Afghanistan. But, caveat is that there are no takers for such a probable regime in international community so it is bound to fail, but it won't allow also the present state to survive and grow stronger.

It is evident that only a stronger economy would render the Afghan state capable of thwarting security breach. This is not possible without international flow of financial resources towards its industrialisation. The investment climate is good with vast mineral resources lay bare to be exploited, but ground situation is hazardous for international companies who would be too scared to risk their vital human resource under such conditions. The January 2014 attack on a famous Lebanese Kabul restaurant took lives of a number of high profile westerners working with international agencies by a blast from suicide bomber and his associate assassins. These killings deliver a high degree demoralising effect to the international presence in Afghanistan. The states of Afghanistan and Pakistan have failed to rein in various shades of Taliban and it makes a threatening scenario only when there is a degree of collusion between the state and the non-state actors. Afghanistan has often accused Pakistan for staging various high profile killings with the help of Haqqani network and the Taliban. On the other, Pakistan accuses Afghanistan for sheltering Mullhah Fajlullah and other Tehrik-i Taliban leaders across border. These have been dealt at one level effectively by drone-warfare, but it has its own collateral consequences. There is dwindling ground support for these operations and the US is getting under criticism from both, the Pakistani and the Afghan side for the loss of lives of innocent civilians. India's security concerns emerge largely from the case of Taliban staging the comeback with its proclivities towards Pakistan's ISI and the Pak army. The scenario is of some concern with the unknown possibility of Al-Qaeda lending its resources to anti-India operations from these regions. These also indicate at extreme threat levels of a possible nuclear adventure by the Taliban and their terror associates. However, it demands at least a greater degree of assistance from Pakistani security establishment, which as a policy decision shall have grave consequences not only for the state of Pakistan, but for the South Asian region at large. It is in the Indian interest that India promotes a cause for democratic statehood in both Afghanistan and Pakistan and maintain cooperation with these governments despite the credibility deficit shown by them on number of instances. Afghanistan has been complainant of hegemonic attitude of international actors who fail to provide funds to state and channelize it through their non-governmental organisations. The international actors respond to it with the lack of accountability and high degree of corruption among Afghan state officials that make any aid programmes ineffective. India has been largely doling out assistance through inter-state agreements. The January 2014 Karzai visit to India brought an additional demand for military hardware for empowering the ANSF. But, the issue of supplies of defence equipment not only involves money, they also have strategic implications. India would be looking for wider regional arrangements to cater to Afghan needs as this would prevent Indian getting sucked into the Af-Pak vortex in case there is rise of conflict to pre-9/11 days. On the other India would like to see a multilateral fora for economic ventures in and across Afghanistan as this would also allow sharing of risk by neighbours and international stake-holders.

1. London Conference to BSA

The January 2014 capture of Fallujah, Iraq by Al-Qaeda led front pointed to the post-drawdown threats quite well. The 2010 London Conference was harbinger to plans for transformation of conflict. The emphasis was upon transformation evolved as the limits to total elimination of threat had already been visible and expectations from the Afghan state were ripe that it would be able to withstand the pressure from Taliban and Al-Qaeda. The drawdown has been conceived as two-fold strategy, first is, to talk with the adversary, and second, to make enough case for deterrence by preparing the Afghan forces. The talks with Taliban meant lowering the counter-insurgency thrust against them, and upgrading military might of Afghan forces with enough provision for their training and armaments that would allow them to take on the adversary. This entailed that Afghanistan's neighbour cooperate in bringing Taliban to table and also provide assistance in raising the Afghan National Security Forces (ANSF). Dichotomously, Pakistan was tasked to bring Taliban to negotiating table, while India was assigned training of the ANSF, as the major goals towards conflict transformation. Latter's co-option in the larger package was an uncanny gesture for the Indian policy makers, who felt bruised by the new found worthiness of Pakistan by the Western interlocutors. The 'trust fund' to lure Taliban in Pakistan was carved out that aimed at persuading them to dissociate with Al-Qaeda. But, over the period, particularly after killing of Osama bin Laden in May 2011, there has been revision of strategies. The US-led NATO decided to keep holing out individual targets, who defined continuum of Al-Qaeda with Taliban groups. The onset of 2014 marked the unwinding of withdrawal process, with full acknowledgement that the US presence would no longer be there to deter Taliban. A proposition feared by many with the return of atrocious rule by Taliban. Afghans have been in principle acquiesced to talks with Taliban and the High Peace Council was exactly tasked for this job. But, with the assassination of Ustad Rabbani in September 2012, it became clear that it would be amiss to expect from supercilious Pakistani establishment to deliver the goods, in fact, obverse became truer in the light of cross-border shelling by Pakistan on both Afghan and Indian side since 2012.

Indian policy makers argued for a strong case of US-led NATO presence post-2014 elections during the London Conference. It has been consistent opinion that current Afghan state is weak in resisting the Pakistani overtures for securing foothold in Afghan government. The case is grounded in history of Pakistan's intervention in Afghanistan where it has tried to exploit its neighbourhood to push in the Taliban and their religious fundamentalism through its so-called strategic assets. India can only rely on Pakistan's goodwill and intent that these two forces are not deployed against its presence in Afghanistan. But, this needs much needed trust between the two, which was unfortunately visible in the later half of 2013 as incessant heavy shelling on both sides. India has been supportive of the Afghan-led and Afghan-owned peace process. The April 2013 Alamaty Conference took Istanbul Peace Process one step ahead reiterating Afghan-ownership of peace process. It also recalled the 'redlines' agreed upon in 2010 London Conference, i.e., to give up all forms of violence, renounce all forms of contact with Al-Qaeda and subscribe to Afghan-spirit imbibed in the Constitution. These are visible elements on which India's foreign policy banks upon. However, there are indeterminate elements that affect India's Afghanistan policy. India's Afghanistan Policy banks upon on five such elements, namely, (1) the Indo-US strategic partnership, (2) the Taliban and the rest, (3) President Karzai and his competitors, (4) the principles of Indian aid and assistance to Afghanistan, and (5) the Indo-Afghan strategic partnership. These are taken up in the following discussion.

2. The Five Factors

The year 2014 elections in Afghanistan would be a litmus test for India's Afghanistan policy. It would establish credentials for a just and stable Afghanistan with commitment towards Constitutional democracy. India would be getting strong policy approval if these succeed along expected lines. The desire to seek stable and secure Afghanistan is a global mandate and one of the important objectives of Indo-US strategic partnership. India has been soft glove to hard fist approach that the US applied in neutralising the Taliban space, which incidentally also coincides with the Pashtun homelands. This has important players on stage of which President Karzai is the most important. In fact, India has banked a lot on Karzai's deep connection with India for its policy vectors. And, therefore, post-2014 elections uncertainties loom over his successor's ability to hold onto the reins of power. The latest and the newest to the kitty is India's renewed considerations towards the Taliban. This is significant as after the Kandahar fiasco, India found Taliban abominable.

2.1. Indo-US Strategic Partnership

India's quest for economic growth and its transformation into global political influence brought significance of closer understanding with the US. The US interest in India emerged with the debilitating of traditional allies, namely, Japan, Philippines and Pakistan, due to internal weaknesses. And, the US believed that the only Asian power that has the potency to be ally in containing China that is India. The most significant was the Indo-US civilian nuclear cooperation that brought a new qualitative change in relationship. India and the US have partnership programmes on economics, energy, defence and terrorism, and also scientific and technical exchanges. The idea of "natural ally" came with the desire to seek enhanced economic success and political goals globally. The quest for strategic autonomy continues to be difficult choice in Indo-US relations. The US changed its perception about India notably on the account of 1998 nuclear tests and then in 2001 the 9/11 attack. It came to realise that India mattered more than mere an ally in terms of its security interest played globally. The problem of weak states in Asia brought India as a necessary ally in the region, which could be extended to Southeast Asia. Indian assistance has qualitative difference to the US engagement in Afghanistan unlike the case elsewhere. India is valued by the US in maintaining the balance of power in Asia. There have been phases of highs and lows largely accruing from the differences of perception. It started during the Vietnam War and then the Indo-Pak wars created the discordant situation. Even the Iraq war was one where the US wanted Indian involvement, but India kept at bay. The Afghanistan war can be no less frustrating even as India tries to limit itself amid growing post-withdrawal uncertainties. The US feels that it needs to keep the Pakistanis engaged into Afghanistan and that would be the sufficient and the most economic case for achieving their desired security objectives. In fact, at no point during the War on Terror, the aid to Pakistan ever dried up. On the other, it increased year on yearly basis.

2.2. India's Relations with Taliban

India was surprised when Mullah Abdus Salam Zaeef was issued visa in November 2013 for Think Fest in Goa, where several Union Ministers were also present. The indications were clear that India was preparing itself to do business with Taliban. This has been more in tandem with Afghan approach to deal with Taliban through High Peace Council, who met Mullah Baradar in Pakistan. But, Afghanistan government has been dealing with Taliban at several levels. At, one level it is the US sponsored peace deal that was initiated under the Qatar process. The second channel is between Afghanistan and Pakistan bargaining with each other in order to secure deal with Afghan Taliban. And, of recent the Pakistan Taliban has started taking shelter in eastern provinces of Afghanistan, viz., in Kunar and Paktia, where they have been used as strategic channel to reach out splinter Taliban groups operating within Afghan territory at the behest of Haqqani network and Al-Qaeda. Pakistan hitherto believed Taliban as strategic asset, but it has serious threat from regional Taliban factions, which are bent upon implementing Shariah in Pakistan. Both, Afghanistan and Pakistan have talked peace with Taliban.

Indian policy makers have to calibrate how far they are going to own this Afghan-owned and Afghan-led initiatives. As, they very much switch over to jihadist mindset time and again with Kashmir on their radar.

2.3. Karzai Factor

India has banked upon President Karzai to carry out its Afghanistan policy. It has been particularly suited as being a Popalzai Pashtun himself, he commands wider legitimacy in society, where traditional structures of power still hold true. Karzai not only is accessible to the intra-Afghan factions, but also to regional partners, such as, Pakistan, India and Iran. This is significant as any post-Karzai presidency needs to command such an in and out influence. The 2009 elections saw Abdullah Abdullah as runner up to President Karzai with 27.8% of votes. It remains to be seen whether he has that nationwide following just like Karzai. But, he would need crucial support from southern Afghanistan and for this he has to seek rapport with Pashtun leaders in the southern Afghanistan and those ensconced in Pakistan. Here the major difference lies in the fact that dealing with Taliban is altogether different where the Constitutional democracy itself is a challenge, that compared to getting other non-Taliban Pashtun-led groups such as Hizb-iIslami and Ittehad-iIslami on board which would give him unique advantage unlike any other into fray for 2014 presidential elections. The coalition under Cooperation Council of Political Parties and Coalitions of Afghanistan (CCPPCA) have brought Afghans closer to Constitutional process by demanding policy actions. President Karzai sees this as a challenge to his authority. And, the fact remains that Taliban is a balancing factor to this duel, which he wishes to secure before 2014 elections. India needs to assess how far it is willing to accommodate Karzai plus 'moderate' Taliban combine, and what would be the impact upon its relation with the former northern alliance members.

2.4. The 'red' Lines

The 'red lines' marked in 2010 London Conference hold much ground for sustained Indian presence in Afghanistan. India's support for democracy and political pluralism effectively mitigates any attempts to monopolise power by one single group in Afghanistan. Indian influence in Kabul could only have greater degree of retention if the Afghan groups remain committed to Constitutional democracy in Afghanistan. It only guarantees better rights to the minorities as enshrined in the Article 4 and Article 22 of the Constitution of Afghanistan. Pakistan's ability to deploy theo-politics has allowed making strategic inroads, often quoted as 'strategic depth syndrome'. Multi-party democracy will act as deterrence to this kind of monopolising of power structure. There is also an important debate on how to deal with Taliban, the talks, whether they mean reconciliation through integration or power-sharing. Taliban, of course, prefers the latter one. This might also bring constitutional democracy under pressure. India has to look how far it can work with these concessions as it has deleterious effect with possible ethnicisation and Islamisation of Afghan society.

2.5. Indo-Afghan Strategic Partnership

A consortium of Indian public and private firms, Afghan Iron and Steel Consortium (AFISCO) successfully bided for Hajigak iron ore mines. The efforts are now on to secure exploration of gold and copper deposits. The economic considerations weigh heavier in post-2014 stabilisation of Afghanistan. Indian firm GAIL signed agreements with Turkmen and Pakistani counterparts for realisation of TAPI can only be seen benefiting Afghanistan, both in terms of resources and revenues. These two reveal that India's Afghanistan policy now need to stage a case for inter-regional cooperation among Afghanistan's neighbours and it includes India-Pakistan rapprochement as well. And, also the intra-Afghan factions need to be shown the merit of peace and prosperity that is much wanted after a three decade long destruction in Afghanistan. India has strategic partnership with Afghanistan in assisting and capacity enhancing of Afghan National Security Forces (ANSFs). However, the December 2013 visit of president Karzai revealed policy challenges for India as he demanded fair amount of combat equipment, which India found difficult to oblige. There is growing acknowledgement that India matters to Afghanistan-Pakistan relationship, just as Pakistan matters to India-Afghanistan relationship.

3. Towards the Constructive Paradigm

The scholars argue that the South Asian regional security complex which has essentially models Indo-Pak conflict extending into Afghanistan in a post-ISAF situation. And, Afghanistan is very much vulnerable to being a turf for settling rivalries between the aforesaid two. Quite in corroboration has been the statement from West Bengal Governor and Former NSA, M.K. Naranayan in January 2014, who cautions that Taliban getting into power would target India drawing latter into the Af-Pak vortex. Both the views are too simplistic to read the current situation and the marked difference 2014 carries with the pre-9/11 days. Both, the analyses take the US presence as a dummy variable, whereas it is the US who has brought all the geopolitical designs in the South Asian region with the obvious help from India. This can only be capitalising if there are stable gains from what the US and India have invested in the region. And, here the geoeconomic content would be hard to ignore, even if Iran gets into the sliver by sheer of its locational importance. India would like to take the initiative on several levels at this juncture. The geoeconomic highways are being conceived in form of India-China dialogue on Afghanistan. The noted scholar on South Asia, Professor Zhao Gancheng at the Shanghai Institute for International Studies stressed the importance for China, India and Russia to work closer on Afghanistan as it will have enormous impact on the future growth scenario for the three countries. The security concerns could be addressed better if the Afghan state is economically rejuvenated and it is possible only with strong economic back-up by India, China and Russia. The US would be bearing larger share of the security costs, and the economic supplement has to be provided by the rest of the three to bring a stable transition in the Afghan situation. There is prima facie case of securing energy transport linkages by India, China and Russia. The TAPI has had hit bottlenecks with Pakistan failing to put enough investments and if China can guarantee the reach of TAPI from Afghan border to Indian border then it becomes a very realisable proposition for all the stake holders. China can facilitate this owing to its charming relations with Pakistan. The NATO and ANSF would prove good enough to secure the Afghan corridor. Also, the IPI pipeline which is an oil-pipeline also has its bottlenecks due to the Iranian nuclear deal. This can be guaranteed if the US remove sanctions to allow its oil companies to be able to pitch in for the financial guarantees and allow the Iranians to extend their credit line to the Pakistanis who would be able to draw in their requirements and make it to the rest of the Indian sub-continent. This would be the two big steps that would eventually make the conflicting state-parties see the point in transforming attitude towards each other. Therefore, a constructivist approach to geopolitical balancing of power is needed. But, this is least of a status quoist approach. India, Afghanistan and Pakistan need to constructively engage each other to take South Asian region on the path of greater political stability. All these targets can be met with synergies of Af-Pak-Ind geopolitical space.

3.1. Geopolitical Constructivism

Pakistan would not like to have Indian influence gain ground even at the cost of sustained insurgency in Afghanistan. The US is looking to Pakistan for long-term formations in the region, which is not in consonance with the Afghan and Indian interests in the region. There is possibility of total pullout amid difficulties in ratifying the Bilateral Security Agreement with the US. This is not all that demoralising scenario, but the lack of strategic clarity of the US post-drawdown is creating ambiguity in regional security dynamics. The US has been consistently supportive of Pakistani establishment with money and arms without much influence over its jihadi framework. India has decided to step up military cooperation with Afghanistan, but at the same it has to face increasingly volatile environment on its border with Pakistan. India's successful contribution to Afghan reconstruction depends on the goodwill of the Afghans; India's relations with the Pushtun groups in the south and Afghanistan's relations with Pakistan. The India-Pakistan rivalry is co-factored into the stability of Afghanistan. Afghanistan's growing frustration with Pakistan is significant contributor to this co-factoring. According to the opinion poll conducted in 2010 by BBC, ABC and German TV ARD, it was found that majority of Afghans wanted India to be in the forefront of reconstruction of the country, while Pakistan was the least popular one. The standing was followed by Germany (59%), the US (51%) and Britain (39%). It was even more remarkable that Afghans rated India's role more and above the agencies such as, the UN and NATO. And, 94 percent people favoured democracy, while only 6 percent favoured the return of Taliban. The poll essentially reflects the approval of Indian approach towards Afghan reconstruction. The political institutions in Afghanistan have been motivated towards democracy and political pluralism, which have been the policy benchmark for all the assistance vectors emerging from Indian establishment. This has obvious discomfort for both, Pakistan and China, its coparcener to the jihadist polity in Afghanistan. India's approach towards reconstruction has not only been governed by the needs of the Afghan state and its people, and how the Afghan State responds to its expectations of maintaining a favourable balance in the South Asian region. India has an important objective of delimiting the strategic depth notion of Pakistan, which it consistently harboured during the Taliban days, as a means to preserve its strategic assets. These assets do not amount to nuclear or ballistic material, but those jihadi elements, which are used by ISI and Pakistan Army to wage proxy war. These purported goals delivered the result during the post-9/11 situation when it was increasingly difficult for Pakistan to maintain levels of support to terrorism in Kashmir. However, as the drawdown nears there is every need to assess these goals in the light of the fact that Pakistan regardless of its relation with Afghanistan would like to increasingly vitiate calm at the Line of Control (LoC).

The important task is then to take stock of how Indian interests can be preserved in post-drawdown Afghanistan. Would the 2014 Afghan elections throw up an increasingly accommodative government in Afghanistan that is willing to increase concessions to Taliban. Or, would there be a regime that decides to confront the cross-border destabilisation emerging from Pakistan. The larger possibility is for latter outcome, but it is a limiting case given there are enough Pushtun groups, who would not like to put their strategic interest in Pakistan to danger. Therefore, India would like to see how the Pushtun groups react to its presence in Afghanistan, especially those entrenched in south. This presumes that there is fair number of chances that some of breakaway Taliban members might enjoin a theo-political alliance which emerges are substitute to present political framework. India would like to see that Haqqani-Taliban-Al Qaeda trio who operate from the tribal regions of Pakistan remain pariah to whatever formation of Afghan state takes place. And, the success of drone in war has Pakistan finding it increasingly difficult to provide unabated support to these groups. Therefore, the multiple Pushtun factions and their matrix in US threat perceptions range them on the drone radar. This has significant bearing on India's relations with Pushtun groups. A very important element is that the non-radical concerns of Pushtun groups define the inter-ethnic balance of power in Afghanistan. The Uzbeks, Hazaras and the Tajiks form a large geo-cultural coalition in Afghanistan, which putatively abhors the accommodation of Taliban on account of being nearly solely a Pushtun led organisation. Therefore, Taliban has also deployed Pushtun rhetoric in justifying its call for political space, which finds subliminal support from non-Taliban Pushtun groups. India has to remain sensitive to this rhetoric as merely being supportive to "Afghan-led and Afghan-owned" does not fulfil the expectations from India, which is the bettered by Pakistan. India would like to see a larger convergent democracy caused by non-Taliban Pushtuns groups along with non-Pushtun Afghan groups in a common acceptable environment. President Karzai relied on this matrix to retain both internal and external balance of power, therefore, it is imperative for India to see through his legacy being carried forward after the presidential and provincial elections in Afghanistan. This can achieved if India relies on the identification of political parties with more inclusive poll manifesto and develop a mechanism with them.

3.2. The Policy Scorecard

India's Afghanistan policy needs to take the following fives' into account for approaching the situation holistically. These parameters are having direct bearing on the nature of Afghan polity. And, if Indian approach vis-a-vis parameters helps in strengthening the Afghan policy then India can remain satisfied with its minimax gains. The table 1 gives a 15 point scorecard for evaluating India's Afghanistan Policy. A comprehensive policy would be one where India's Afghanistan policy carries the Indian intent in the region. And, it can also give a preferential ordering of the elements which India would like to promote in Afghanistan and demote those which India thinks can grow into regional harm.

Table 1: Scorecard for India's Comprehensive Afghanistan Policy

A	Structural Challenges	Indian Policy Vectors
1	Corruption	Support for Strengthening Parliamentary Democracy
2	Depleting Aid & Assistance	Multi-lateral Investment Policy
3	Training of ANSF	Promote UN and SCO mandate for ANSF training
4	Ethnic strife	Support for ethno-political pluralism
5	Reconciliation with Taliban	Support for Afghan-led and -owned process
B	Policy Tiers	Policy Inertia
6	India-Pakistan relations	Insurgency and Cross-border terrorism
7	India-US relations	Drones and the Af-Pak paradigm
8	Afghanistan-Pakistan relations	Durand Line and the Haqqanis
9	Afghanistan-US relations	BSA and Pakistan's involvement
10	US-Pak relations	Negotiating with Taliban
C	Social Grounding	Transformative Elements
11	Non-Taliban and non-Pushtun groups	Support for Karzai's broadbased approach beyond 2014
12	Pro-Taliban Pushtuns and Constitution	Support for Constitutional and Legal Framework of State
13	Hazaras as litmus case	Check, their Political Identity remains secure
14	Kuchis as litmus case	Check, their Economic Position betters
15	Women as litmus case	Check, Women and Girl Child Rights are secured

These 15 odd elements provide handles to augment various situational responses in the wake of ebb and flow of Afghanistan's political stability. Based on these parameters a survey was conducted among the thinkers and intellectuals in Kabul, a 25-point score was given to them to scale all the 15-point factors based on their significance for India's Afghanistan Policy. They necessarily reflect the Afghan concerns, but linking them with an external variable leads them to assess the factors, which are exclusively domestic while others as external which India can identify for its Afghanistan policy. The significance of factors was tested by conducting factor analysis and Eigenvalues were taken as criterion for selecting those factors which explain maximum degree of impact on score. It may not reflect the true weightage of individual loadings, but when a combination of factors that are identified through the analysis gives fair idea about the expectations from India.

A set of six factors were found out to have Eigenvalues above one. These factors together explain 80 percent of the variance. The results as follows:

Fig. 1: Scree Plot for 15 Factors under study

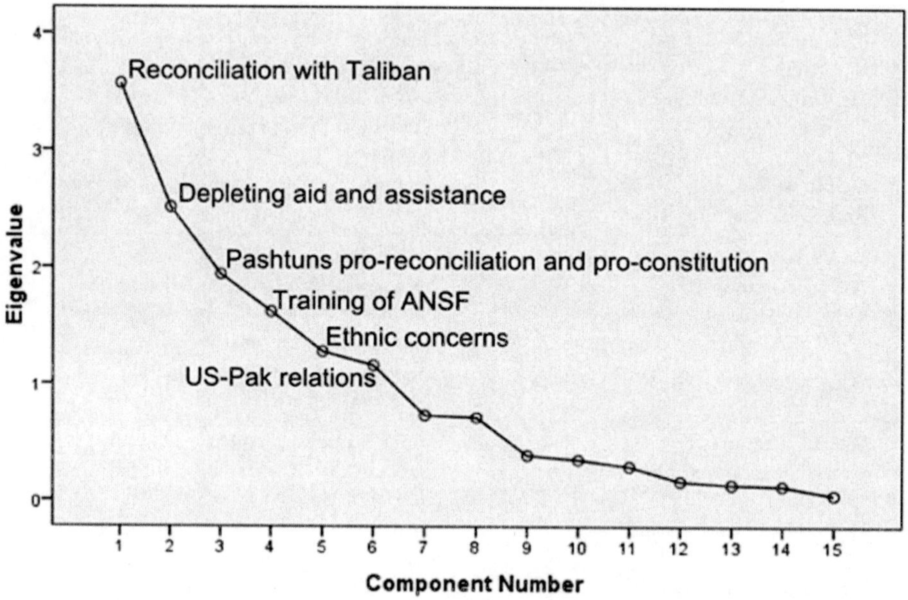

1. Most of the respondents believe that the most significant factor is the reconciliation with the Taliban (factor 5). It alone gives 23.8 percent score among all the factors.
2. Next important factor is 2, which identifies aid and assistance to be tackled by the multi-lateral investment policy. It carries 16.7 percent loading among all the factors.
3. Third most significant factor (12) is pro-Taliban Pushtun, who definitely wish to get Constitutional democracy in Afghanistan as well. This might carry only 12.9 percent loading, but has great importance for India's Afghan policy.
4. The fourth significant factor that explains a very significant concern is the ability of the Afghan forces to defend their territory. Therefore, training of ANSF (factor 3) scores a high attention in this regard. This has nearly 10.7 percent loading. The sum of aforesaid set of four factors explains 64 percent of total phenomena that are currently vital for Afghan population.
5. The other two factors are with eigenvalues greater than 1 are the ethnic balance in the Afghan state (factor 4) and US-Pakistan relations that can help deliver peace for Afghanistan (factor 10).

These results can be sourced into recommendations as follows:

1. Most Afghans believe that India must pay attention to the reconciliation process with the Taliban. Whether this indicates that India must join a Qatar process, or India should initiate its own process of negotiating with Taliban remains to be seen. But, it is for sure that for India to have a successful Afghanistan Policy it cannot simply bank upon the rhetoric of Afghan-owned and Afghan-led process. India has to ensure that there some tangible gains for it too.
2. The investment in Afghanistan is the second most important factor. Here, India would do well if BRICS can be brought into realm. The entire BRICS community has reputed oil companies and it has financial muscle to guarantee their investments. Therefore, India must get multi-lateral partnerships in Afghanistan rather getting a home-knit alliance of public and private partnerships.
3. Third factor is very delicate but a very significant one. This essentially reflects that a majoritarian perspective is to be built and it is necessary for the identity of Afghanistan. But, it must have a wider acceptability to the plural minorities of Afghanistan. Therefore, India must acknowledge President Karzai in his initial years had to face is as an enormous challenge, i.e., to de-Talibanize the Pashtun identity; and his legacy needs to be preserved in all the successive relations between India and Afghanistan.
4. The fourth factor call for India's consistent support to ethnic pluralism, democratic governance and just law. That would retain the trust of all the ethno-nationalities into the Constitution. This is the sole-2014 guarantee that can bind them together under all adversities. So, India must endeavour to reinforce Parliamentary democracy in Afghan politics.

There is fair degree of indication that for India to have a successful Afghanistan policy it has to take into confidence all those Pashtun-led political groups who stand for political pluralism and are averse to any monopolising force (including Taliban) bent upon capturing the Afghan state. Karzai approach has been vital as it attempted to strike balance between India and Pakistan so far as stability is concerned. Therefore, the Indo-Pak talks on Afghanistan at some stage have to materialise for a tangible Afghanistan policy. The nationalist character of ANSF is important while empowering it with material and technical capabilities. Therefore, their increasing role in training them helps India to better address its Afghanistan policy. Corruption in Afghanistan has the potential to disrupt ethnic balance of power. The resources differential may cause serious rifts among ethnic groups. If the Bilateral Security Agreement is signed, the US forces would continue to put pressure on Pakistan to deliver the necessary goodwill in its favour. These are some of the accepted factors that lend India a meaningful Afghanistan policy. India needs to sharpen its approach along these lines and a mere case of humanitarian approach is not going to suffice its strategic needs.

13

Afghanistan post-2014: Implications for India and Indian Options

Alok Bansal

As the US pulls out of Afghanistan, there are apprehensions about its future. Many in the West believe that the current political dispensation in Kabul will not be able to hold on its own against the Taliban onslaught. Accordingly the US had proposed positioning a small US military detachment, which could help the Afghan troops in times of dire need. This could also be used to build up American military presence expeditiously, in case the demise of the democratic dispensation in Afghanistan appears imminent. Unfortunately, the Bilateral Security Agreement (BSA) between the Afghanistan and the US has got mired into politics. On the other hand Pakistan is trying to convince the Western world that a lasting peace in Afghanistan is unlikely without co-opting Taliban.[1] A weary American administration, which desperately needs a face saver, is buying the Pakistani argument. Numerous attempts are being made to negotiate with the Taliban, which are in no way contributing towards peace, but are weakening the foundations of current Karzai administration in Kabul.

India and Afghanistan have a long historical relationship and barring the Taliban regime, the two countries have shared cordial relations. The security and stability in Afghanistan is essential for the regional security and therefore for India's growth and stability. It is therefore important for India that radical Islamic organisations with a global agenda do not get entrenched in Kabul. 2014 is going to be a significant year for Afghanistan, as President Karzai will complete his two terms and secondly, at least the bulk of US and NATO troops will pull out from the country. The future of Afghanistan to a great extent thereafter will depend on the security guarantees and financial support that the country receives from international community. The way things shape out will have a direct impact on India's security. It is therefore in India's interests to ensure that the events in Afghanistan shape up in a manner that they do not threaten India's long term security and interests. This paper looks at the future of Afghanistan after 2014, its impact on India and the options that are available with India to ensure that Afghanistan remains stable and secure.

Afghanistan post-2014

Afghan presidential elections, of April 2014, restricts the presidential terms to only two terms and hence the incumbent president Hamid Karzai could not contest the 2014 elections. Ten candidates were in the fray, but only five were believed to have any worthwhile chance of getting elected. These top five contenders according to analysts were Abdullah Abdullah, the runners up in 2009, Zalmai Rasool, former minister of foreign affairs, Ashraf Ghani Ahmadzai, former foreign minister, who also ran in 2009, Abdul Rab Rassoul Sayyaf, an Islamic scholar and Abdul Qayum Karzai. It is generally believed that the whole imbroglio over BSA is primarily because the President wants to retain his influence and wants to ensure that the next president is someone he approves of. In fact other than Abdullah Abdullah, all the other four top candidates are believed to be obliged to him. He has virtually ensured that at least one of these will be in the run off. The grapevine in Kabul is that President Karzai will nudge the candidates who don't make the run-off to back his preferred candidate to ensure his relevance and continued influence in future Afghanistan.[2]

President Karzai's behaviour is probably governed by his desire to prevent the US from interfering in 2014 elections the way they did in 2009. Now that Robert Gates has admitted that the US diplomats had connived in delaying an Afghan presidential election in 2009 and had tried to manipulate the outcome so as to oust President Karzai, his intentions of keeping the US focussed on BSA may be justified.[3] For the 2014 elections to be credible, it is essential that external powers must not meddle in the election process besides sending in the observers to ensure a free and fair election. The successor to President Karzai will face the serious challenges of a flourishing trade in narcotics, a fragile economy, an inefficient and corrupt administration and widespread insurgency in rural areas. However, for him to be successful his election must be credible without any external interference. While, the new President must have good relations with the international donor community, he must not be perceived to be a stooge of external powers.

Even more significant than the elections is the fact that the US and NATO are slated to pull out bulk of their forces from Afghanistan by 2014. The United States has proposed retaining around 8000 troops in Afghanistan after the pull out to support the Afghan National Army (ANA). The presence of US troops is expected to provide the decisive psychological edge to the government against the Taliban. To facilitate the presence of these troops the US is insisting upon Afghanistan to sign the BSA. Initially President Karzai indicated that the decision on BSA would be taken at Loya Jirga, which was attended by 2,500 of Afghanistan's influential citizens from throughout the country. After three days of debate, the loya jirga overwhelmingly endorsed the BSA as written and urged President Karzai to sign it before the end of the year.[4] He however, made fresh demands and suggested that the agreement could be signed by his successor. Among his new demands, include the release of Afghan detainees from Guantanamo Bay.[5] The delay could jeopardise all the commitments of assistance to Afghanistan including its security forces.

The future stability in Afghanistan depends on the Afghan National Security Forces (ANSF), which primarily include the Afghan National Army (ANA) and the Afghan police. Of these the ANA is the key to Afghanistan's survival as a modern state and its success or failure will shape the state's destiny. Many in the West perceive it to be a rag-tag militia, incapable of sticking together, much less fighting the Taliban. It may well have been the case in the initial years after the fall of Taliban, when various components of ANA were trained by different western countries. However, the ANA has come of age and although it may not be comparable to other armies of the region, it is now fairly cohesive, notwithstanding the occasional desertions. It has already taken over the security responsibility for most of the country. Most of its constituents have a pathological hatred for Taliban. It is therefore not likely to crumble as many in Pakistan and the West believe. Many believe that the 352,000 strong ANSF are too large and will require $6.5 billion annually to keep them intact, whereas only $3.6 billion was pledged during the Chicago conference in May 2012. It must however, be appreciated that $ 6.5 billion is the western estimates and roughly equals Pakistan defence budget, which caters for 1.4 million personnel including 500,000 reserves and 300,000 paramilitary personnel and possesses a much larger and sophisticated inventory of arms and ammunition including ships and aircraft. Although the annual budgetary estimates of ANSF have been reduced to $ 4 million, it should be possible to maintain the ANSF at a much lesser cost, if the pay and perks are based on South Asian norms.

According to the latest reports, funding support for transitional period of five years from 2014 has been committed by the US and its allies for the ANSF. However, there is a world of difference between the commitment and the payment and many in the West are calling the force levels to be unsustainable and asking for its pruning down. Western propensity to route its aid to the Afghanistan through Non-Governmental Organisations (NGOs) could further aggravate the financial problems of Afghan government. It must however, be clearly appreciated that the ANSF have to be manpower intensive to fight the insurgency and any demobilisation at this juncture will be counterproductive. However, the ANSF and especially ANA, needs to be trained and equipped well. Under sustained pressure from Pakistan, the ANA has not been equipped well. It has neither been provided with multirole combat aircraft to create a credible Air Force, nor with heavy artillery. While it is not intended to use them against insurgents, they would provide crucial psychological edge against non-state actors in a civil war. More significantly, they would work as insurance against cross-border interventions. As regards training of the ANA, it has definitely improved, but its desertion rates indicate that it still has to cover a lot of ground, before it can evolve as a stable and cohesive army. Some estimate that the attrition rate could reach as high as 40 percent by the autumn of 2014.[6] The biggest problem has been that the western trainers have not understood the cultural ethos of the orient and that is precisely the reason behind most of the Green on Blue attacks in Afghanistan.

Implications for India

Many of those occupying positions of power in Islamabad and Rawalpindi have for long cherished dreams of controlling Afghanistan after the US withdrawal. They perceive that as soon as the last US soldier departs from Afghanistan, the Taliban will raise its flag on Kabul and as far as Pakistan's interests are concerned, Mullah Omar will continue to be as accommodative as he has been during his stay in Pakistan. Even though this premise is highly flawed, the very idea threatens India. From India's point of view, any presence of an obscurantist radical outfit like Taliban within the power structures in Kabul, threatens India's security and it is therefore essential that India must have a proactive policy to ensure that an independent and strong Afghanistan capable of keeping Taliban at bay, emerges after withdrawal of the troops from United States and its allies.

India has invested heavily in Afghanistan's infrastructure. It has built roads, powergrids and dams. It has also established hospitals and schools. All these would come to a nought if a regime hostile to India captures power in Afghanistan. Many of India's companies have invested in mining projects in Afghanistan and all this investment could be jeopardised if the Afghan state is not secure and stable after the departure of the US and NATO from 2014. Similarly India has lot of hopes from Turkmenistan Afghanistan Pakistan India (TAPI) Pipeline to India's bourgeoning energy demands. However, instability in Afghanistan will make the prospects of TAPI Pipeline ever fructifying extremely remote.

More significantly, it is often forgotten that today's Taliban is closely aligned with the Global Islamic Movement and notwithstanding the recent postulations from Mullah Omar; it is still being manipulated by the Al Qaeda. Its aims and objectives are no longer confined to the geographical frontiers of Afghanistan and it eventually aims towards the creation of a global Islamic Emirate. Al Qaeda cadres believe that they are fighting 'End of Times' battle in Khurasan,[7] which will be followed by Ghazwa-e-Hind (a term used in Prophet's saying and means battle for India).[8] Today Taliban shelters radical

Islamists from all parts of the world and these hardened warriors will move to newer battlefields in case Taliban establishes itself in Kabul. One of the likely battlegrounds where many of them could move is Kashmir and hence establishment of a Taliban regime in Kabul will directly affect the level of violence in a Kashmir.

The rise of these elements in Pakistan thus poses a direct threat to Indian security as the current phase will be followed by attacks on India. Its presence at the helm of affairs in Kabul will not only divert the plethora of global Islamic militants fighting there to other countries in the region, but the Taliban regime could also provide material support to these radical organisations. It is therefore in India's interest to fight these radical organisations, which are striving to establish a transnational Islamic entity in Afghanistan rather than on Indian Territory. Consequently, the war against Taliban is not only Afghanistan's battle, but also a key ingredient of India's quest for security.

Indian Options

In order to formulate an objective policy, certain prevalent myths need to be dispelled. The British, as the former colonial masters of South Asia, have succeeded in selling to the Americans a highly flawed narrative of the Afghan History. Consequently, terms like "graveyard of Empires" have come to symbolise Afghanistan. The truth is Afghanistan as an independent state is a recent entity, and for centuries under the Mughal rule, Kabul was ruled from Delhi. More significantly, even though, Afghanistan was not colonised, it has never been free from foreign influence or interference and this state has persisted to this date. Secondly, it must be remembered that the last communist regime under President Najibullah held on to power for three years after the Soviet withdrawal in 1989 and collapsed only because its vital supplies of ammunition and POL were disrupted, after the collapse of the Soviet Union. Besides, both Pakistan and the United States did not fulfil their treaty obligations and continued to arm the *Mujahideen*. After the withdrawal in 2014, one does not visualise Americans pulling out to the last man a la Soviets, despite all the hitches on BSA. It would therefore be reasonable to presume that they would continue to maintain their toe hold and retain the capacity to build up forces expeditiously. This factor alone will boost the confidence level of the regime and play a major role in strengthening it. India should therefore mediate between the US and Afghanistan to ensure that all the hitches involved in signing of BSA are removed.

It is widely believed in Afghanistan that the country is best suited to train its forces is India, which not only has a highly professional army and good military infrastructure, but also understands the cultural sensitivities of the orient. According to various opinion polls in Afghanistan, India continues to be the most popular country in the entire region. Consequently, Afghanistan's first Strategic Partnership Agreement was signed with India on 04 October 11, which allows India to train and equip ANA.[9] However, the current practice of bringing Afghan personnel for training to India, not only increases the cost, but also restricts the number and the duration for which they can be trained. Ideally India needs to set up training facilities in Afghanistan with Indian training teams for imparting necessary skills to the personnel from ANA. In the past, India's reluctance to put boots on ground in Afghanistan has reduced Indian leverage with the West. While it may not be necessary to get involved in a conflict with Taliban on Afghan territory, it would be extremely desirable to set up training establishments in Afghanistan, preferably in Hazarjat, which does not border any other country and has a population which is extremely hostile to Taliban. These facilities will help the ANA to emerge as a force to reckon with, which can not only expel Taliban from Afghanistan, but can also keep the Pakistan Army tied up on its Western borders should the need arise. These training establishments will also enable India to retain its influence on the ANA for a long time.

India has been amongst the largest aid givers in Afghanistan and Indian aid has been considered to be the most effective, both by the Afghan government and the population, yet India has not been able to derive proportional influence from its aid. This has primarily been on account of the fact that the security in Afghanistan was being looked after by foreign troops and India had no security presence in the country, this is likely to change with Afghans looking after their security. India also needs to provide military hardware to ANA to bolster its capabilities. Many of the older guns, armoured vehicles and aircraft, which are serviceable, but do not meet the growing aspirations of India's military could just be gifted to Afghanistan along with the maintenance facilities. First and Second Line maintenance facilities for such equipment could also be set up on the Afghan soil by Indians. In addition provision of indigenous military hardware like Advanced Landing Helicopter Dhruv or Light Combat Aircraft Tejas to Afghanistan could be considered. Afghan pilots can continue to train in India as hitherto. All these would create long term relationships between the two countries.

In the non-military field, India should strive to takeover some Provincial Reconstruction Team (PRT) in North or Central Afghanistan. Paramilitary forces like ITBP could be deployed for the protection of Indian nationals involved as part of PRT. As PRT work will be geographically limited. This should be relatively easier than protecting them across entire length and breadth of Afghanistan. Afghans by and large cherish past Indian contribution in the field of education and health, and want more Indian education and health care facilities to be set up. They could therefore be set up initially in the secure North and Central Afghanistan and subsequently, in other parts. These would allow India to influence large population, gain goodwill, as well as to contribute to the process of de-radicalisation of the youth. Colleges in Afghanistan could be affiliated to Indian Universities allowing them to imbibe their secular curriculum.

Many analysts perceive that India should evolve a joint strategy with the Central Asian States to counter the Taliban and Pakistani influence in Kabul, but it has the grave disadvantage of being perceived as anti-Pakhtoon in Afghanistan's fractured ethnic mosaic. Similarly, any coalition with Iran is likely to be perceived as anti-Sunni by the dominant sect in Afghanistan. In addition, considering the tenuous nature of US-Iran relations, any relationship with Iran has a risk of running afoul of the US. The best option for India is to bank on ANA and pro-India politicians in Afghanistan. India must not allow it to be side-lined on Afghanistan as was done in Turkey and London Conferences. There are many Afghan politicians who are willing to do India's bidding.

Indian business and industries, both public sector as well as private sector, must be encouraged to invest in Afghanistan and to exploit the vast mineral resources of the country. There is however, a problem of access as minerals extracted have to traverse through a long route via Iran to reach India. It may be worthwhile to consider the option of transporting them through Xinjiang in China. China like India faces grave threat from Taliban and its global Islamic affiliates. It is therefore keen to collaborate with India to prevent Taliban, which has close relations with Uighur militants, from coming to power. India needs to understand that failure in Afghanistan is not an option and Taliban in Kabul is akin to Taliban at Wagha and poses an extremely grave threat to India's existence as a thriving secular democracy.

END NOTES

1. Murtaza Ali Shah, "Taliban must be part of peace, political process, says Nawaz", *The News*, October 30, 2013, Karachi Edition, p. 1.
2. Ioannis Koskinas, "'Who's Who?' A Primer on Afghanistan's Presidential Candidates" from http://southasia.foreignpolicy.com/posts/2013/11/25/whos_who_a_primer_on_afghanistans_presidential_candidates (accessed on January 11, 2014)
3. "US 'tried to oust Hamid Karzai by manipulating Afghan elections'" fromhttp://www.theguardian.com/world/2014/jan/10/us-hamid-karzai-afghan-elections-robert-gates (accessed on 10 Jan. 14)
4. The Opening Statement of James F. Dobbins, Special Representative for Afghanistan and Pakistan before the House Foreign Affairs Committee on "U.S.-Afghanistan Bilateral Security Agreement" on December 11, 2013.
5. Karen DeYoung, Ernesto Londoño and Kevin Sieff, "Karzai is unlikely to meet deadline on signing long-term security deal, U.S. envoy says" from http://www.washingtonpost.com/world/national-security/karzai-is-unlikely-to-meet-deadline-on-signing-long-term-security-deal-us-envoy-says/2014/01/09/2a9f01fc-7957-11e3-b1c5-739e63e9c9a7_story.html (accessed on 10 Jan 14)
6. S Iftikhar Murshed, "Afghanistan and the wages of inaction", *The News*, Karachi Edition, January 13, 2014, p. 6.
7. Khurasan refers to parts of Iran, the Central Asian Republics, Afghanistan and parts of Pakistan.
8. Syed Saleem Shahzad, *Inside Al-Qaeda and the Taliban: Beyond Bin Laden and 9/11*. London: Pluto Press, 2011, p. xvi.
9. "India-Afghanistan Relations" from Govt of India Ministry of External Affairs Website www.mea.gov.in/Portal/ForeignRelation/afghanistan-aug-2012.pdfý (accessed on 10 Jan 2014)

14

India's Security and Strategic Concerns vis-a-vis Pakistan's role

Rana Banerji

Even as US forces scaled down their presence in Afghanistan to 84,000 by the end of 2013, uncertainty persisted about their continuance in Afghanistan after 2014, whether in a professed non-combatant role or in special operations mode. The 'zero option' threat given by President Obama may not be carried out if the Bilateral Security Agreement (BSA) can be concluded with the Karzai government in Afghanistan but the extent, location and role of the international forces remains in doubt.

As of early 2014, the security threat inside Afghanistan is assessed as follows: 28% in the East, 23% in the South, 38% in the South West, 3% in the West and 1% in Kabul. After 2014, while ANSF may be able to hold its own in the main cities the Taliban would definitely resurge in the rural areas, especially in the south-east, south and south west.

U.S.-Afghanistan Strategic Partnership Agreement

On April 22, 2012, Afghanistan and the United States finalized the US-Afghan strategic partnership agreement (SPA), which has a duration of at least 10 years and lays out the framework for a future American role in Afghanistan, including aid assistance and governance advice, covering areas. One of the provisions of the agreement is the designation of Afghanistan as a major non-NATO ally of the United States. It went into effect on July 4, 2012.

BSA Impasse

However, the status of U.S. troops and details of their operations after the withdrawal of NATO forces were to be covered in a separate Bilateral Security Agreement (BSA), to be signed within one year. Negotiations dragged on between the Americans and the Karzai administration to outline what would be their legal status, operating rules and where they would be based (9 or 10 bases like Bagram, Shindand or additionally fortified units in or near Kandahar have been mentioned), whether they would be in a professed non-combatant role or in special operations mode.

After announcement of plans by the US to engage in peace talks with the Taliban in Doha, Qatar, the Taliban opened what amounted to an embassy-in-exile, complete with their old flag and a plaque with their official name, "The Islamic Emirate of Afghanistan." This enraged President Karzai and he temporarily suspended these discussions (June 19, 2013). Talks faltered again in recent months over the Afghan government's insistence that the United States guarantee Afghanistan's security and, in essence, commit to declaring Pakistan as the main obstacle in the fight against militancy in the region.

U.S. Secretary of State John Kerry and Afghan President Hamid Karzai announced on October 12, 2013 that they reached an agreement on a set of core elements of the bilateral security.

Karzai Calls for 'Loya Jirga'

However, agreement on providing immunity from prosecution under Afghan law for American troops who remain in Afghanistan after 2014 remained elusive. President Karzai announced at this stage that this issue would be decided first by a traditional gathering of elders known as a loya jirga and then be ratified by the Afghan Parliament. Though the draft framework agreement included demands for protection of Afghan sovereignty and rules on how military operations were to be carried out on Afghan territory, the one issue outstanding was the issue of jurisdiction. The other main sticking point was sharing of intelligence.

Karzai refused to allow American forces to hunt for operatives of Al Qaeda here on their own. Instead, he wanted any intelligence gathered by the United States handed over to Afghan forces, who could then conduct the raids. The final language of the bilateral security agreement specifies that U.S. forces will be "cooperating in training, advising, and assisting" Afghan forces "in a targeted, smaller, counterterrorism mission." The agreement qualifies that "unless mutually agreed, United States forces shall not conduct combat operations in Afghanistan". United States Special Operations forces will retain leeway to conduct anti-terrorism raids on private Afghan homes. American counterterrorism operations will be intended to "complement and support" Afghan missions but US forces will not conduct military operations in Afghanistan "unless mutually agreed."

The agreement text grants the United States full legal jurisdiction over U.S. troops and Defense Department civilians working in Afghanistan. On troop immunity, it says that Afghanistan agrees "that the United States shall have the exclusive right to exercise jurisdiction" over members of the force and its civilian component "in respect of any criminal or civil offenses committed in the territory of Afghanistan. "Afghanistan authorises the United States to hold [civil and criminal] trial in such cases, or take other disciplinary action, as appropriate, in the territory of Afghanistan, but Afghan authorities can ask that anyone be taken out of the country. Afghan authorities are prohibited from detaining American troops or U.S. civilians working with them. In the event that happens "for any reason," however, those personnel "shall be immediately handed over to United States forces authorities." The agreement also specifies that American troops and civilians cannot be surrendered to any "international tribunal or any other entity or state" without express U.S. consent. Afghanistan retains legal jurisdiction over civilian contractors, and contractors are prohibited from wearing military uniforms and "may only carry weapons in accordance with Afghan laws and regulations."

US military and Defense Department civilian personnel would be exempt from visa requirements and taxation. Afghan taxes and other fees will not be imposed on the entry or exit of goods specifically for the use of U.S. forces.

Loya Jirgah Approves BSA with Conditions

The loya jirga set a few conditions before expressing approval for the agreement, among them a 10-year time limit on the post-2014 troop presence and reparations for damages caused by U.S. troops deployed in Afghanistan. It also voted to attach a letter of US President Obama pledging that U.S. troops would enter Afghan homes only in "extraordinary" circumstances and only if American lives were at direct risk, to the text of the BSA. They also demanded the release of 19 Afghans from the U.S. detention center at Guantanamo Bay and a stronger U.S. pledge to defend Afghanistan from any incursion from its neighbours, particularly Pakistan. The loya jirga's Hazara delegates requested that an additional U.S. military base be added to the 9 already envisaged, in Bamiyan Province.

Karzai's 'signature' Spanner

After endorsement of its terms by the Loya Jirga, President Karzai surprisingly qualified that the agreement would not be signed until after 2014 Presidential elections in Afghanistan. American officials have been unequivocally insisting that the agreement must be signed by the end of 2013, if not sooner, to allow the Pentagon to prepare for its role after the American combat mission ends.

Officials of the Obama Administration consider the signing date to be non-negotiable, citing the need for at least a year to plan future deployments and to allow coalition partners, including Germany and Italy, to plan for a residual troop presence that they have offered. After visiting Kabul and holding discussions with President Karzai, Amb. James Dobbins, U.S. special envoy for Afghanistan and Pakistan, indicated in a press conference that he had failed to make any breakthroughs on the stalled BSA. According to Dobbins, both sides stuck to their positions. Earlier attempts to break the deadlock, by U.S. Secretary of State John Kerry and National Security Advisor Susan Rice also failed. As Dobbins headed back to Washington, Sen. Carl Levin (Democrat), the chairman of the Senate Armed Services Committee, issued a letter to President Obama urging him to stop insisting that Karzai sign the BSA and wait until his successor is chosen in next April's presidential election. Levin went on to say that the administration's actions "contribute to President Karzai's mistaken belief that the United States needs Afghanistan more than Afghanistan needs the United States." (This is the first time that a top Democrat in Congress had taken a stance other than that being pursued by the administration, which has not commented on the letter).

On December 08, 2013 US Defence Secretary, Chuck Hagel visited Kabul. Though he met his counterpart, Afghan Defence Minister, Bismillah Khan, he did not meet President Karzai. This is being seen as a deliberate snub and a view crystallising in USA that there was no need to keep begging Karzai to sign the BSA. The new deadline for signing which is emerging seems now to be the NATO review meeting in February, 2014. If there are no signatures even then, USA could be forced to use the 'zero option', withdrawing all troops by the year end.

2013 has probably been the most violent year since 2001. The number of war dead has increased again, foremost among the civilian population. According to the UN, civilian casualties increased by ten per cent (to 2,730 dead and 5,169 injured). The Taliban now attack in larger groups more often. They have increasingly attempted to take over district centers, mainly in peripheral areas, and test the power of the Afghan National Security Forces (ANSF). The ANSF now operates on its own in most areas. Only five of the 416 district centers are under Taliban control, but in many others government control barely reaches beyond the immediate urban centre. In the key Maiwand district in southern Afghanistan, for example, it ends two kilometres outside its central town. The situation is similar other key districts, for example in Chahrdara in Kunduz province, from where the Taliban had been driven out almost completely earlier in 2010. Since the additional US 'surge' forces left the area (the last German soldiers withdrew from Kunduz in October 2013), the Taliban are back in control there.

Uncertainties over Afghan Presidential Elections

Presidential elections which were to be held in Afghanistan in April, 2014 saw delay in passing laws for re constituting the Independent Afghan Election

Commission (IEC). The process of issuing new electoral identity cards (e-tazkira), new voter registration cards and lists were not completed.

Political polarisation came to bear in the election, given the absence of sufficiently independent institutions and a body of arbitration. The basis for renewed manipulations in 2014 already existed since President Karzai rejected the cancellation of older, fraud-prone voter registrations cards and their further increase by a new round of voter registration in 2012–13 and with the large discrepancy between the estimated number of voters and the number of distributed voter cards. Immediately before the 2010 poll, there were 17.5 million distributed voter cards. At the same time, the IEC estimated 12.5 million voters. The UN estimated there should be only 10.5 million voters. According to UNDP's election project in Afghanistan ELECT II (updated 22–30 November 2013), now 3.2 million new voters were added, putting the total number to 20.7 million. This raises questions of accuracy as Afghanistan has a total population of 27 million in mid-2013, half being of non-voting age (under 18 years).

According to a recent joint opinion poll conducted by ATR and TOLO news, residents from across Afghanistan's 34 provinces answered questions regarding their preferred Presidential candidates. Results from this opinion poll show that Dr. Abdullah Abdullah is leading, with 27 percent of respondents. In second and third place respectively are Dr. Ashraf Ghani Ahmadzai with 19 percent and Qayoum Karzai with four percent. Presently, the political transition process, with the presidential election in 2014, stands on a shaky foundation. Governments "would do well to plan for a messy election

Pakistan's Motives

While it professes to work for a stable Afghanistan and inclusive government, with power sharing between diverse ethnic actors, in practice the Military Establishment remains confident in its belief that the Taliban would be a manageable proxy, if and even after it can be assured a predominant share in the post-2014 power dispensation in Kabul. The Pakistanis have been reluctant to allow Americans direct access to senior Taliban leaders inside Pakistan, whether in free safe havens of Quetta Shoora or Miramshah/Peshawar Shuras or whether in their own 'protective' custody.

Reconciliation Process

Yet, optimism on chances of reconciliation resurfaced after two meetings, one in Paris in mid-June, 2012 and the other, a seminar in Kyoto, Japan, June 29, 2012 where Afghan government representatives were able to interact with nominees of the Taliban-Qari Din Mohd, ironically enough a Tajik, and Siddique Mansoor Ansari of Hizb-e-Islami (Hikmatyar) attended the Kyoto seminar.

Doha Office Opening Fiasco

According to claims made by a Pakistani journalist known to be close to Army Chief, Gen Kayani, months-long painstaking and secret negotiations involving Islamabad and Washington yielded a detailed roadmap for steering negotiations with the Afghan Taliban. The opening of the Taliban office in Doha, Qatar, was to be but one of the many elements of a complex process, the ultimate aim of which is for all stakeholders in Afghanistan to share power through an inclusive election process under a possibly modified Afghanistan Constitution.

Karzai strongly objected to the Taliban's office in Doha styling itself as a mission of the Islamic Emirate of Afghanistan. In a vocal protest, he suspended talks with the United States on the strategic security deal for continued presence of US troops in Afghanistan after 2014. Washington tried to calm him down and down played the Taliban attempt to show that their office in Doha was a diplomatic legation recognized by Foreign Powers.

The breakthrough in negotiations came through personal diplomacy between John Kerry and Pakistan's then Army Chief, Gen Ashfaq Parvez Kayani. The two had an excellent equation even before Kerry became Secretary of State. Pakistan claims also to have facilitated a quiet and effective dialogue process between the non-Pashtoon forces (the Northern Alliance) and the Taliban in which the two sides at a senior level agreed to bury the hatchet and work jointly for stabilising Afghanistan. Pakistan claims, this was a big breakthrough because this made the peace efforts truly all-inclusive and curtailed the voices of discord and divisiveness that could have raised questions about Pakistani motives.

Factions and Rifts within Taliban

Serious differences have been reported between Maulvi Zakir of the Peshawar Shoora and Mullah Akhtar Mansoor, who claimed to be Mullah Omar's deputy. Emergence of second string leaders within the Taliban has seen squabbling over reform edicts ('Layha')—how much concession to make on issues like allowing girls schools to continue or girls up to a certain age to go to existing schools in burqas (veils). Younger field commanders of Taliban appear much more hardline and reluctant to make accommodations in the reconciliation platform. Morae issues may surface in right earnest if Taliban ultimately open talks at Doha. New power struggles could develop between the senior leaders of Taliban and second string Commanders. Question marks persist over the unease in relations between the Quetta Shoora commanders based in Quetta and Haqqani network fighters in Miramshah.

Nasiruddin Haqqani Killing

Nasiruddin Haqqani, a senior leader and financier of the Haqqani network was killed in Islamabad on November 11, 2013 in a shooting incident as he and two others were driving a car. He is the fourth senior Haqqani network leader killed in the past two years. Three others—Mullah Sangeen Zadran, Badruddin Haqqani and Janbaz Zadran were killed by US drone strikes. Nasiruddin might have been the victim of a tribal feud within the large Zadran tribe, whose homeland in the southeastern Afghan provinces of Khost, Paktia, and Paktika. Zadran tribe members had previously broken ties with the Haqqanis because of their association with Pakistan. In addition, Haqqani fighters have targeted tribal leaders and terrorized villagers. Recently slain Pakistani Taliban (TTP) leader, Hakimullah Mehsud had turned against the Haqqanis because of their long-standing alliance with Pakistan's powerful military establishment. The Haqqani sanctuary in North Waziristan is threatened by this deepening rift, also with Hafiz Gul Bahadar, a powerful Pakistani Taliban leader. Bahadur and his supporters are unhappy with

Nasiruddin's brother, Sirajuddin because of his support for radical fighters from Pakistani Punjab.

Post-Kerry Visit Developments

During the visit of new American Secretary of State to Kabul, despite seeming accommodation of several of Karzai's contentious demands-over handing over of prisoners in Bagram, and 'Afghan-led' process in next elections, Kerry could not quite wrap up the Status of Forces agreement. A joint report was presented by Pak ISI and MI to the Supreme Court alleging that Afghanistan may be instigating terrorist incidents in FATA/ Khyber Pakhtunkhwa through persons like Mullah Fazlullah and Faqir Mohd. Though this report was classified, it seems to have been deliberately leaked to the media.

Kabul also alleged unprovoked firing by Pakistani forces across the border in Kunar. In an interview to Reuters, Afghan Foreign Ministry official, Javed Ludin, Deputy Foreign Minister condemned Pakistani doublespeak and alleged that Pakistan was not only undercutting the Karzai government but also playing off the various non-Taliban groups against each other. The scheduled visit to Pakistan of an eleven member Afghan Military delegation to the Staff College, Quetta was cancelled.

The ISI is believed to have developed influence over second string field commanders in southern Afghanistan. Using Afghan refugees based in Pakistani camps, they have introduced them as Soviet style 'commissars' into these provinces, to work closely under Taliban commanders. They provide finances to the Taliban leaders. Their families are given Pakistani citizenship.

Insurgency safe havens remain inside Pakistan though the threat itself may reconstitute, depending on the extent Afghan Taliban are facilitated to partake of the power sharing cake, in case the negotiation process with them finally gathers momentum, albeit with of or control by Pakistani State actors. Anthony Cordesman of the Center for Strategic and International Studies, USA said recently, "Pakistan is not going to stop interfering in stability in the region. In a report by Seth Jones and Keith Crane, the US Council on Foreign Relations—Centre for Preventive action suggests that Pakistan is unlikely to change its support to Afghan insurgents in the near term. US policy makers are advised to become less dependent on Pakistan while dealing with the post-2014 situation in Afghanistan.

Capacities of ANSF

There are many problems with the quality of the ANSF. Its fighters' motivation remains low, its composition is ethnically unbalanced and it lacks logistical abilities. Their procurement procedures are corrupt. The Ministry of Interior —known for its systematic sale of positions completely stopped its anti-corruption reforms. Desertions and other forms of attrition are high and combat losses are rising. After 2001, the US government cancelled conscription in Afghanistan, against the will of President Karzai. As a result, the ANSF's recruitment capacities were undermined. The role of the armed forces bringing young men from different ethnic backgrounds together also slowed down. One third of all ANSF personnel must be replaced every year. Networks linked to the former civil war militias penetrate the army and police; soldiers and policemen often are more loyal to their former armed factions than to the central government.

The simultaneous establishment of the militia-like Afghan Local Police (ALP) shows that Western donors mistrust the regular ANSF. The ALP with its 23,551 fighters in 115 areas of the country (as of July 2013), composed of former civil war militias that have escaped disarmament and insurgents that have switched sides is already the fourth militia generation since 2001. It increasingly has become a problem itself. In a report to Congress on progress in the war, the Pentagon asserted that "overall security has improved in most villages" where ALP units patrol but according to a secret study commissioned by the US Special Forces command in Afghanistan that trains, monitors and supplies the ALP, every fifth ALP unit is involved in the drug trade, extortion of illegal taxes, land grabbing, murder, rape, running secret detention facilities and violent internal power struggles. In Kunduz, the creation of the ALP in communities where social fractures or ethnic frictions are salient has fostered rather than appeased tensions [and] the population is caught between the lines of fire of two warring parties. The confrontation between the ALP and the Taliban adds a layer of conflict in the quasi-civil war being staged.

The end of the ISAF mission and its replacement by a pure training mission may be coming too early, given the state of Afghan institutions, including the armed forces. Many of the deeper lines of conflict existing in Afghanistan have not been tackled—from ecological and demographic aspects to the economic marginalisation of the country in the neo-liberally globalized world.

Effectiveness of Pakistan's anti-Indian Strategies in Afghanistan

The other overpowering Pakistani consideration is to limit India's role and presence in Afghanistan, at best to development activities sans any political clout on the power brokers who emerge in Kabul. Pakistan vociferously opposes a robust Indian role in Afghanistan or U.S. support for such a role. Islamabad perceives India's efforts to gain influence in Afghanistan as a deliberate strategy of encirclement that is aimed also at instigating and intensifying the persisting insurgency in Balochistan.

Attacks were carried out against the Indian Embassy in Kabul twice, in July, 2008 and October, 2009 as also on the Indian Consulate in Jalalabad in August, 2013. Militants suspected to belong to the Haqqani network coming in from Pakistan were involved. A Kabul rest house where Indian doctors working in Indian medical missions in Afghanistan stayed in transit was also targeted.

Security and Strategic Implications for India

Even in the future, as assessed in a 2012 Rand Corporation occasional paper by Larry Hanaeur and Peter Chalk, Pakistan could retaliate against India with political, economic, and military pressure by taking one or more of the following steps:

- blocking Afghan exports to India, most of which currently cross Pakistani territory;
- pulling out of an arrangement to construct a regional pipeline that would transport natural gas from Turkmenistan to Afghanistan, Pakistan, and India and continue pursuing a bilateral pipeline with Iran in its place;

- turning increasingly to China for assistance with military, commercial, and infrastructure development assistance, which could further impede Indian initiatives to project power in South and Central Asia; provide additional military capabilities that could be used against India in an armed conflict and frustrate Indian efforts to counter Chinese influence in the region;
- most critically, encouraging attacks on Indian interests in Afghanistan, escalating insurgent activity in Kashmir, or supporting Mumbai-style terrorist attacks, any one of which would cause a steady stream of Indian casualties and generate significant domestic political turmoil in India.

Evolving Scenarios in Afghanistan—2014 and Beyond

Three possible scenarios could be envisaged post-2014, one in which there is maximum Taliban influence in the power dispensation which emerges in Kabul—this would be the best case option for Pakistan, also it would be acceptable to USA if Pakistan guarantees good behavior of their proxies; the second case could be of inclusive power sharing by all ethnicity players/ power brokers/old warlords. Pakistan is increasingly paying lip service to this option now. However, this option may be unstable and could lead to increasing civil strife. The third option would be the worst case scenario, of enhanced civil strife and renewed fighting between all the warlords and the Taliban.

Implications for India

The first option would have the most dangerous implications for India, reducing our influence in Kabul and jeopardizing the scope of our continuing development assistance programmes in the country. A somewhat alarmist interpretation also holds possibility of Afghan territory again serving as nurturing ground for terrorists/militants who could be sent into Jammu & Kashmir. However, Mullah Omar has declared in his recent messages that the Quetta Shoora would not allow any activities detrimental to other countries from Afghan soil. Whether they can live up to this promise and withstand or reject Pakistani pressure in this regard remains to be seen.

The other two options presage instability and increasing civil strife, which cannot be very good for India or even Pakistan. Other regional power brokers would come into the picture as well in such scenarios. In the ultimate analysis, India should remain prepared to continue its diplomatic and developmental engagement in Afghanistan, with whosoever comes to power there, depending also on the nature of relationship and requests for assistance that are received from the new government there. As back up options, India could consider reviving old friendships in an uncertain power equilibrium and even think of cultivating new Pashtun friends, if these are of moderate hue and eschew radical links. In sum, Afghanistan beyond 2014 promises many uncertainties which would require India not to become complacent yet remain ready with flexible and balanced responses.

15

Impact of Afghan Drawdown on Kashmir

Tareak A. Rather

The NATO pull out from Afghanistan in 2014 will be one of the most significant geopolitical shifts in the beginning of this century. The fact of the matter is that USA has not won the war on the battlefield, nor has the country ended the conflict on the negotiating table. The Americans are simply washing their hands off it. What is of great strategic significance for us is that post–US situation does not degenerate into an India-Pakistan battlefield. The likely withdrawal of NATO forces has aroused lot of policy and media attention and security experts too have joined to assess as to how things will shape up in and around Afghanistan. In recent times this has aroused curiosity in Pakistan and India as well.

What is of strategic relevance for us is the manner in which Afghan situation has factored in the security calculations of managers of Indian state as far as Kashmir is concerned. Many security experts and army officers posted in Kashmir have been talking about it and are suggesting that there can be no lowering of guard in Kashmir. India and Pakistan are at strategic crossroads and will have to turn Afghan situation into an opportunity for better engagement rather estrangement.

Syed Atta Hassnain (former general officer commanding of the Srinagar-15 corps) in an article in Indian Express (victory in the Valley 11 December

2013) argued that Kashmir is far too complex for inexperienced minds to fully comprehend and there are so many stakeholders it confounds even those who have a semblance of it. We have to measure victory against a realistic assessment of the future. Mr Atta Hasnain was responding to media discussions on demilitarisation in the valley considering the fall in violence and successful elections conducted here.

Within the valley there are voices cautioning against the growing drift and frustration with lingering conflict. In many of very important conferences it has been made clear that hopelessness in Kashmir can prove a very destabilizing factor which can wash out gains accrued of earlier peace process. Chief Minister of the state Mr. Omer Abdullah on July 13, 2013 expressly stated that highly qualified youth in Kashmir have started joining militancy and it is a matter of concern. They apprehend that lack of a structured dialogue may trigger what they refer to as spill over of Afghan war into Kashmir. Whatever, the objective realities the fact remains that there is already a psychological siege within Kashmir and this can be largely attributed to a clear vacuum on the ground.

On his return from Pakistan in 2012 Hurriyat Conference chairman Mirwaiz Omer warned that violence in Afghanistan will spill over if steps are not taken to resolve the Kashmir issue. In his first press conference after return from Pakistan he stated that the coming year and half was very important. He saw the issue to be a window of opportunity for India and Pakistan to come together for the solution of Kashmir issue. Mirwaiz's comments echoed former top army commander Atta Hasnaian who had already said that 2014 will be crucial for Kashmir. On 17 April 2013 Jammu& Kashmir Liberation front Chairman Yasin Malik said the withdrawal of NATO forces from Afghanistan has a potential to change the discourse in Kashmir as people may think that non-violent movement had failed and gun was the only way to resolve issues. He also made it clear that our movement is indigenous and it will continue to remain so".

On April 8, 2013 PDP patron and former Home Minister of India Mufti Syed called for safeguards for J&K from hazardous fallout from Afghanistan. Observing that unstable conditions in the state could make it prone to negative influences. Mufti further asserted that we need to create an atmosphere of hope in J&K. A US military report titled: *The fighters of Lashkar-e-Taiba: Recruitment, Training, Deployment and Death* also warned in April, 2013 that some of the Pakistan-based militant groups like LeT, backed by elements in Pakistan establishment will reorient and invest more broadly in the conflict in Kashmir post-2014 American drawdown.

The above context suggests that Afghan situation is quite fragile and vulnerable to all sorts of influences. Every one having stakes in the stability of larger region must contribute towards making Afghanistan free of all external interventions. None of the key players can afford another civil war. The fighting could easily turn into a regional proxy war. India and Pakistan should be able to find a common ground much easily in Afghanistan than Kashmir. Disorder in Kabul serves neither of them.

In the month of July, 2013 Indian Foreign Minister did a fine balancing act when he rejected Afghan arms plea. Salman Khursheed stressed that we are going to help with non-lethal equipment but I don't think we are either in the position to or willing to contribute lethal weapons right now". Ahmed Rashid-author and journalist writes: India and Pakistan need to institute a series of bilateral meetings on the Afghan situation at several levels, from the diplomatic to intelligence and military. Such talks would make their missions more transparent and create greater trust. Much greater openness is needed on issues such as the number of intelligence agents each embassy maintains in the country and the alleged support given to Bloch dissidents by India and to Taliban fighters by Pakistan.'

Hence any way forward must take into account not only internal stability in Afghanistan but greater stability in India-Pakistan relations. Equally essential is to begin a meaningful dialogue on Kashmir and not pushing it into too hard category and leave it to simmer. All this can be done by taking three purposeful initiatives and factoring them in any future policy instrument on Afghanistan:

1. Improve internal situation within Pakistan
2. Resume India-Pakistan Dialogue process
3. Consolidate gains and mapping the future course of Action in Kashmir

However looking at the number of militants killed and arrested from last four years, as per the police records not even a single militant was an Afghan national. The foreign militants killed were mostly Pakistani Nationals. According to police sources Hundred thirty four militants are present in the valley: LeT–68, HM–32, Albadar–01, JeM–3.

Table 1: Number of Militants Killed during 2010-1013

Year	*Foreigners*	*Locals*	*Total*
2010	115	48	163
2011	57	21	78
2012	49	15	64
2013	46	16	62

Table 2: Number of Militants Arrested during 2010-1013

Year	*Foreigners*	*Locals*	*Total*
2010	01	99	100
2011	01	125	126
2012	0	150	150
2013	02	62	64

Source: J&K police Headquarters' Srinagar.

However reluctance of army to withdraw AFSPA even from those places where army has not carried any operation from last four years serves no body's purpose. The Chief Minister's consistent demand to New Delhi for its withdrawal at least from Jammu and Srinagar districts has fallen flat due to army's opposition. Speaking to media on Jan. 13, the Chief of Army staff Genral Bikram Singh said, "there should be no dilution of AFPSA in J&K in view of the prevailing situation in the region, including possible militant spill over into the valley after US drawdown in Afghanistan. We need to look at developments in Afghanistan in 2014 before we can look at perhaps tampering with or diluting AFSA in J&K." This pushes mainstream politicians against the wall and brings cheers in the separatist camps, which leads to further alienation of the masses".

The recent floods (7th September) in Kashmir have brought untold miseries on the people both in Jammu and Kashmir region and it is for the first time from last two and a half decades that the socio-economic narrative has replaced the political narrative. Meanwhile Election Commission of India decided that elections will be held in J&K in November and we witnessed a huge turnover (70%) in first phase (25th of November). This huge turnover of voters particularly the youth has proved all political pandits and security analysts wrong who had started ringing the alarm bells once US decided to withdraw its forces from Afghanistan.

Conclusion

The change of government in Delhi and Prime Minister Modi's invitation to all the heads of the states of SAARC countries and Prime Minister Nawaz Sharif's participation despite army showing reservation raised lots of hope in Kashmir. People of J&K thought that this government meant business and has absolute majority may start a new chapter of cooperation, and will take steps to overcome the trust deficit which both countries accuse each other. But this was very short lived as India decided to call off the secretary level talks, on the pretext of Pakistan High commissioner meeting the *Hurriet* leadership at his residence in New Delhi. If anybody had still doubts about that talks won't be deferred for two long the 18th SAARC Summit held in Kathmandu were the two heads of the state didn't even had a single eye contact despite sharing same stage for two long hours has put these doubts to rest. Prime Minister Narendra Modi's reference to 26th November Mumbai attack in his speech which incidentally was the date of 6th anniversary of those killed said Our wounds have not healed yet and we feel endless pain of loss of lives" and Prime Minister of Pakistan's reference in his speech that "we are ready for the talks but India has to take the initiative" summed the mood of the two heads of the state's. One tends to believe that the diplomatic war of two neighbours regarding Kashmir may unfold in Afghanistan in near future. How India will respond to the whole twists and turns of Pakistan's diplomacy regarding Kashmir and Afghanistan remains to be seen.

16

Indian Engagement in Afghanistan (Post-2001): A Critical Analysis

Saurabh Kumar

American security establishment received a rude jolt on the 11th of September in the year 2001. On that day, Al-Qaeda carried out a series of coordinated attacks on several important installations across America. They used civilian airliners as their medium and ended up claiming around three thousand lives. The American military administration and its intelligence wings were caught completely off-guard. With a view of taking swift and devastating retribution, the American government initiated a series of acts that would finally result in a United Nations approved, though not sanctioned military intervention in the Taliban controlled state of Afghanistan. This event also sowed the seeds for India to engage with Afghanistan, after a long and conspicuous absence post-Soviet withdrawal and Taliban takeover.

Initiation of Conflict

The US led Afghan intervention did not receive any formal authorisation from the UN. It was widely believed that such an action was legally tenable as the UN charter authorised armed action with the final aim of self defence. It could claim legal protection when a competent organ of the UN, mostly the Security Council authorised it, or where it was in self-defence under article

51 of the Charter[1]. US and UK led the charge that the Taliban government in Afghanistan was protecting the Al-Qaeda led by Osama Bin Laden and hence led the plans for an imminent military action. Security Council Resolution (UNSCR) 1386 of December 2001 allowed for stationing of an ISAF force of a strength of 5000 personnel in and around Kabul for the purpose of reconstruction and security under chapter VII of the UN charter[2]. They were duly mandated under the UN charter but not controlled and supervised by UN leadership as it was stated by Lakdar Brahmini while signing the Bonn agreement that formation of a UN controlled force was time taking and would work only if there was any kind of pre existing political agreement between the parties in dispute i.e. the ISAF led forces and the Taliban or any other major stake holder in Afghanistan, which was clearly absent in this case[3]. This arrangement of providing security via ISAF continues to exist in present day, in the year 2015. While it can be reasonably argued that with the creation of an Afghan government that was elected by Afghan people under a popular mandate, a UN supervised force could be created, but nonetheless all the stakeholders in this mission have preferred status quo, with ISAF having become a major player in the region.

India-ISAF Collaboration

After the American led ISAF forces were given due mandate to intervene, Indian involvement began as a subsidiary partner who helped the ISAF gain entry into Afghanistan with some deal of intelligence, logistical and transport help. India has viewed a stable neighbourhood in Kashmir to be linked with a stable Kabul and Afghanistan. The chaos following Soviet military intervention and subsequent withdrawal after a long and bloody war in the year 1989 bought Indo-Afghan relations to a standstill. With the collapse of Soviet Union, India had a tough task in hand trying to create a new and effective foreign policy and thus they ignored and neglected the events that were transpiring in Afghanistan. The Taliban dominated post-Soviet Afghanistan and took over the nation in 1996[4]. Indian ties with Afghanistan hit nadir throughout the Taliban's 7-year rule, but India tried to maintain its presence by supporting the Northern Alliance by providing money and material. But when US led forces intervened and were able to overthrow the regressive Taliban regime, India with its then enhanced economic, political and military power found a way to resume its diplomatic relations with Afghanistan[5]. According to reports, these were the different kinds of help that India rendered to the ISAF forces initially when the military action in Afghanistan started—

1. Providing naval frigates for escorting coalition ships through the Straits of Malacca[6].
2. Local shipyards helped in repairing coalition ships[7].
3. Local ports were available for naval port calls[8].
4. Indian intelligence officials provided the United States with information about financial and training sources of Islamist terror groups in Afghanistan and Pakistan[9].
5. Indian government also offered its territory and military bases for carrying out operations in Afghanistan against terrorist and insurgent elements[10].

Though miniscule and token, this help did in a way help India regain trust of major NATO and ISAF powers that they were willing to contribute themselves in rebuilding strife torn Afghanistan. This generated the initial goodwill for Indian assets to be placed in Afghanistan for assisting West and ISAF forces rebuild and stabilise the strife torn nation with deep ethnic divisions.

Indian Interest in Rebuilding Afghanistan

India's primary aims at securing Afghanistan are linked to[11]—

1. Securing a peaceful neighbourhood and ensure violence and humanitarian crisis do not spill over like the IC 814 hijack incident. India aims to ensure that radical groups do not take over the reins in Afghanistan, as they did in the year 1996 as it can put the entire region in turmoil.
2. Ensure radical groups in Afghanistan do not support similar groups in Kashmir.
3. Energy security from central Asia and reduce dependence on Persian Gulf region, which is politically volatile as well.

Indian Engagement with Afghan Government under Karzai

Hamid Karzai's election as Afghan President, first by a Loya Jirga in 2002 and subsequently by the Afghan people in 2004 and 2009 consecutively led to a long and productive Indian involvement in Afghanistan[12]. Hamid Karzai was widely known for his pro India stance as is indicated by his rapport with Indian leaders especially then PM Dr Manmohan Singh. He had a personal connection with India as he was educated here[13]. Diplomatic relations were further bolstered by close cultural and historical ties between the two countries.

Indian aid to Afghanistan has had these three typical features[14]—

1. Indian projects are located in almost every part of Afghanistan, in a wide range of sectors.
2. These sectors have been decided by the Afghani government as priority areas for reconstruction and development.
3. These projects have been undertaken in conjunction by the two governments with great emphasis on local ownership of assets and are a part of a long drawn Afghanistan National Development Strategy.

In a 2008 joint statement on Hamid Karzai's visit that came a few months after the devastating terror attack on the Indian embassy in Kabul, India re-affirmed its staunch commitment to Afghanistan by citing that,[15] "India's commitment to Afghanistan would be fully met. To this end, the Government of India pledged an additional 450 million US dollars over the 750 million US dollars announced so far to effectively meet the requirement of our ongoing and forthcoming projects". In effect, in the year 2008-2009, India was contributing around 1.2 billion dollars on reconstructing Afghanistan. This shows the deep financial burden that India has been undertaking to help Afghan masses have access to the most basic and necessary facilities that were mostly absent till then. This as per some recent figures has escalated to as high as 2 billion dollars[16].

Indian contribution has been widespread and diversified. It can be best highlighted with the following sets of achievements in different fields—

(I) Humanitarian Assistance[17]—

1. Daily supply of 100 grams of fortified, high-protein biscuits to nearly 2 million children under a School Feeding Programmeas part of the World food programme.

2. In order to help Afghanistan deal with its food crisis, India allotted 250,000 metric tonnes of wheat in January 2009.
3. India provided free medical consultation and medicines through five of its medical missions in the cities of Kabul, Herat, Jalalabad, Kandahar and Mazar-e-Sharifto, benefitting over 30,000 Afghans monthly.
4. India rebuilt Indira Gandhi Institute of Child Health in Kabul. It is currently the largest paediatric hospital in Afghanistan. India has also been engaged in capacity building of Afghan doctors by allowing several batches of IGICH specialists train at the All India Institute of Medical Sciences, New Delhi.

(II) Major Infrastructure Projects[18]—

1. Construction of 218 km road from Zaranj to Delaram to facilitate movement of goods and services from Afghanistan to the Iranian border and, onward, to the Chabahar Port
2. Construction of 220kV DC transmission line from Pul-e-Khumri to Kabul and a 220/110/20 kV sub-station at Chimtala to bring additional power from the northern grid to Kabul
3. Construction and commissioning of Salma Dam power project (42 MW) in Herat province
4. Indian engineering teams have built an all new Afghan national parliament in the capital city of Kabul.
5. Restoration of telecommunication infrastructure in 11 provinces
6. Expansion of national TV network by providing an uplink from Kabul and downlinks in all 34 provincial capitals for promoting greater integration of the country

(III) Education and capacity development[19]—

1. Reconstruction of Habibia School, Kabul.
2. 500 annual long-term university scholarships Construction of the Zaranj-Delaram Highway sponsored by the Indian Council for Cultural Relations for under-graduate and postgraduate studies for Afghan students in India.
3. 500 annual short-term ITEC training programmes for Afghan public servants in Indian technical and professional institutions of their choice.

4. The Indian government deputed around 20 civil servants as coaches and mentors under Capacity for Afghan Public Administration (CAP) programme supported by UNDP and the Governments of Afghanistan and India.
5. India-Afghanistan Vocational Training Centre for training Afghan youth in carpentry, plumbing, welding, masonry and tailoring has been undertaken under supervision of the Confederation of Indian Industries.
6. Women's Vocational Training Centre in Bagh-e-Zanana for training of Afghan women (war widows and orphans) in garment making, nursery plantation, food processing and marketing, executed by the well-known Indian NGO SEWA (Self-Employed Women's Association).
7. Capacity building programmes have been extensively undertaken in the diverse fields of diplomacy, media and information, civil aviation, agricultural research and education, health care and medicinal science, tourism, education, standardisation, rural development, public administration, electoral management and administration, and local governance.

(IV) Security assistance—

Indian involvement in this arena has been relatively sparse and limited to mostly non-lethal aspects, thus helping Afghan security forces in these ways—

1. India has given non-lethal military equipment worth $3 million to shore up the Afghan National Army (ANA).[20]
2. India has been training Afghan soldiers in small batches in different military schools. This process has accelerated post the vital 2011 SPA i.e. Strategic Partnership Programme Agreement that seeks to allow India to train and equip Afghan security forces.[21]
3. India has provided Afghan Army with non lethal military instruments like vehicles, cutters, bullet proof jackets bullet proof posts, medicinal equipmentsetc.[22]
4. Under a deal with the Russian government, India has supposedly decided to pay Russia for artillery, helicopters, guns, etc. that Afghanistan intends to buy for them. India will also deal with the financial costs of up keeping them. Thus, rather than providing

Afghanistan with arms and ammunition, India has rather chosen to pay for them.[23]

5. India has also provided the nascent Afghan Air Force with 3 HAL Cheetal Light helicopters as a part of military aid.[24]

Afghan Perception about India and Indian Aid

Indian support for the Northern Alliance against the Pakistan-backed Taliban in the 1990s helped it immensely in the post-Taliban period in Kabul after 2001. Many members of the Alliance ended up holding key positions in the federal government in Kabul or at the provincial level. India has tried to restore the balance in its engagement with a range of different ethnic groups and political affiliations in Afghanistan. This has yielded impressive results for India[25].

As per a 2009 poll conducted by ABC and BBC news channels, general perception about India amongst Afghan populace is overwhelmingly positive, with about 74 per cent of the surveyed individuals stating that they regarded India highly[26]. A diplomat has also been quoted saying "this is the first time I have been in a country where Indians are appreciated simply for being Indian"[27]. Afghan citizenry has welcomed Indian involvement in development projects in their country; Indian films and television programs are extremely popular among the local Afghan populace, and India is amongst the top favourite destinations for Afghans with its embassy and four other missions issuing around 350 visas daily[28].

India has become a preferred destination for medical tourism for wealthy Afghans. There has been a spurt in the number of flights between the two national capitals as more and more Afghans come to India for trade and professional activities[29]. Afghanistan chose India for its "first ever" strategic partnership which also shows the extent that ties have deepened amongst the two countries and reflects the positive perception about India[30]. The current Afghan president, Ashraf Ghani has also termed India as an "all weather friend"[31]. "Hindustan Hamara dost" which roughly translates into—India and Afghanistan are friends, is a popular chant in Kabul[32]. Indian popularity is across ethnicities with Tajiks, Hazaras and Pashtuns having a very positive reaction to its involvement[33]. This in spite of the fact that India at one junction supported the Tajik dominated Northern Alliance in the years 1996-2001. This shows about Indian engagement being fair and focused on Afghanistan as a collective entity and not some groups and regions at the cost of the rest.

However, it is also to be noted that the change in leadership in Afghanistan could change things for India. Ashraf Ghani is also trying to spruce up things with China and Pakistan[34] in order to accelerate peace and growth in Afghanistan which may not be approved by some Indian policy makers. This uncertainty can be cleared once Ashraf Ghani visits India in April, 2015. His visit can help understand the future roadmap of Indo-Afghan relations and the possible role India can be expected to play in near future.

Response from International Community

Indian engagement being extensive, has garnered a mixed bag of interesting responses from different members of the international community—

> In my paper, I would like to limit that analytical portion of responses to chiefly two sets of international community-the first being Pakistan and secondly, western forces especially US and UK, who are engaged extensively in Afghanistan and hold the key cards there.
>
> While arguably, they have worked together, but for different reasons. The west wants to stabilise Afghanistan to ensure that it does not become a hot-bed for terror again while for Pakistan, it is a reluctant war against its still preferred ally, the pro Pakistan factions of Taliban.

Response from Pakistan

India's engagement with post-Taliban Afghanistan was suspiciously viewed initially by the United States, Pakistan and the Afghan government to be a strategy to undermine Pakistan. But on the contrary, India has come to accept that Pakistan has different interests that overshadow its own. Primarily the Indian government aims at preventing the return of an Islamic state government that could provide strategic depth to Pakistan and Kashmiri militants than setting up a government in Afghanistan that has proximity towards Delhi more than Islamabad[35].

Pakistan was once called as Afghanistan's "twin brother" by former president Hamid Karzai, who emphasised on a good relationship between the trioka of India, Pakistan and Afghanistan for a stable and peaceful neighbourhood[36]. It has a long standing border with the country and is used by NATO forces primarily for transportation of important items, though of late US is turning up to other Central Asian countries for the same.[37] Pakistan had helped America immensely in driving the Soviet forces out by helping different anti Soviet fighters who were called "Mujahideens" or holy fighters[38]. As a result US has remained indebted to Pakistan and has acted accordingly to keep it in good humour. Pakistan has been accused of trying to derail Indian aid by organising ferocious attacks, like the 2008 Kabul embassy attack by using the Haqqani brothers controlled terror network[39]. Pakistani officials have articulated deep concern about what they view as dangerous and growing Indian encroachment in Afghanistan. Islamabad has accused the different Indian missions and consulates in Afghanistan of waging a proxy war by supplying Baluchistani separatist and insurgency groups with weapons and other materials—though without publicly offering any evidence to substantiate the claims. In addition, Islamabad views Indian support for the development of Iran's Chabahar port which could provide a route for Indian trade with Afghanistan as competition with Pakistan's new Chinese-built port at Gwadar[40].

Pakistan feels that because of the proximate historical and cultural links that existed between Afghanistan and Pakistan since medieval times, any attempt by India to infringe upon this "bond" is an attempt to hurt the ties that have existed between the two countries for long. They feel that Pakistan being an immediate neighbour holds greater rights in rebuilding and stabilising Afghanistan and that Indian aid is nothing more than a strategic encirclement. India providing arms to Afghan military can further turn the atmosphere rabid and can only worsen matters in the conundrum[41]. Pakistan has thus repeatedly accused India of making matters worse in Afghanistan by indulging in a wily game of deceit and lies. A great deal of Pakistanis thus deeply resent Indian involvement in that country as a result.

Afghanistan with TTP and Baloch separatist has been termed by some groups in Pakistan to be a part of India's "great game" to break Pakistan down and "subjugate" them to Indian domination. This "great game" is because India supposedly sees Pakistan as an impediment in its efforts to dominate south East Asia and that India is insecure of the close "all-weather ties" that China and Pakistan share[42]. Pakistan as a result feels that India's insecurities have manifested via such anti Pakistani actions, especially with regards to Pakistan. Several of them feel that India needs to restrain its involvement and cede greater ground to Pakistan for managing Afghanistan better and also stop its proxy war aimed at breaking Pakistan down.

Some analysts also feel that India should take into account Pakistani interests and work out some kind of joint strategy towards stabilising and rebuilding that country. This is because both countries have a lot at stake in rebuilding Afghanistan. China can also be an important factor for the two countries to focus on while rebuilding Afghanistan[43]. This middle path that has also been supported by several members of the international community like USA, UK. They feel that the two most important members of the Indian sub-continent can work out with China and stabilise the region jointly by getting over mutual dis-trust.

If Pakistan feels threatened by Indian involvement in Afghanistan, they could retaliate using one or more of the following steps[44]:

1. It can completely restrict/block Afghan exports to India, most of which currently cross Pakistani territory and thus force Afghanistan to search for an alternate route.
2. It can pull the plug on the plans to construct a regional pipeline that would transport natural gas from Turkmenistan to Afghanistan, Pakistan, and India and continue pursuing a bilateral pipeline with Iran in its place. It has the potential to hurt India's energy security plans in the future.
3. It can ask its "all weather friend" China for assistance with military, commercial, and infrastructure development assistance, which could further impede Indian initiatives to project power in South and Central Asia and also provide additional military capabilities that could be used against India in an armed conflict, and frustrate Indian efforts to counter Chinese influence in the region.
4. Most critically, it can encourage targeting of Indian interests in Afghanistan, and escalate insurgent activity in Kashmir, or support Mumbai-style terrorist attacks, any one of which would cause a steady

stream of Indian casualties and generate significant domestic political turmoil in India.

However, it is to be pointed out that Pakistani fears do appear un-warranted because of the following reasons—

1. Indian help to Afghanistan is not region or ethnicity specific.[45]
2. Indian help is with complete collaboration of Afghan government.[46]
3. Indian help is primarily concerned with socio-economic development of Afghanistan.[47]
4. Indian help has been acknowledged and appreciated as genuine by several world leaders, including Barrack Obama in his Delhi visit in November, 2010, which indicates the kind of positive impact Indian involvement has had on Afghanistan.[48]

Response from West

India, because of its strategic location and involvement has been given the sobriquet of "the sponge that protects" the West[49]. Western countries have acknowledged Indian contribution to Afghanistan and its role in stabilising the country to some extent. However, they have refrained from allowing or asking India to contribute boots on the ground with the view that security operations are being best handled by Western forces that make up a great majority in ISAF. However, there is seemingly no consensus among leading ISAF contributors like US and UK about what India should do in the event of violence in Af-Pak region spilling over to its own soil[50].

Western countries have often tried to ignore or completely discard Indian opinion with regards to managing ground affairs in Afghanistan. It was seen in the 60-nation London conference on Afghanistan in January 2010, which advocated talks with the Taliban that shocked Indian diplomats. When Indian External Affairs Minister S.M. Krishna underscored the folly of making a distinction "between a good Taliban and a bad Taliban," he was seen as being a sore thumb at the conference. This was greatly because US and other western partners of ISAF were willing to get out of the Afghan problem by trying to woo back "moderate" Taliban back into power in Kabul with the help of ISI and Pakistani military[51]. In May 2012, Washington and Kabul signed a strategic partnership agreement, which will lead to the Afghan security forces taking the lead in combat operations by the end of 2012; all American combat troops will be leaving by the end of 2014. This will not include trainers, who will assist Afghan forces and a small contingent of troops with a specific mission to combat al-Qaeda through selected vital counterterrorism operations[52].

US has also obliged to Pakistani demands with regards to managing Afghanistan because of fears of retaliation by Pakistan by a combination of one or more of the following means[53]—

1. Pakistan could provide even greater support for the Afghan insurgency than its current provision of safe-haven and operational assistance to the Taliban.
2. Islamabad could continue to block supply convoys en route to U.S. troops in Afghanistan from passing through its territory, as it has done several times before. A long-term prohibition on shipping supplies across Pakistani territory could complicate U.S. logistics efforts, particularly those supporting the withdrawal of U.S. combat forces and material from Afghanistan; the United States would be dependent on the longer, more costly, multi-nation Northern Distribution Network (NDN). But, with alternate central Asian routes coming up, this measure may not yield much in the future.
3. Islamabad could retaliate by withholding counterterrorism assistance, particularly regarding Taliban and al Qaeda fighters and facilitators finding safe haven inside Pakistani territory. To date, however, such cooperation has been considered to be inconsistent and unreliable. But of late the west has also tried addressing India's concerns. The Kabul embassy attack was blamed on the ISI by the US administration who also admonished them for their insecurities[54]. US president Barack Obama, as has been pointed out before appreciated Indian help in Afghanistan categorically during his Delhi visit in the year 2010[55].

US also slapped sanctions on Haqqani brothers, a terror outfit that has targeted Indians in Afghanistan and enjoys patronage of the Pakistani establishment. This shows that of late, western countries have begun sharing Indian concerns as well[56].

Shortcomings of India's Afghan Policy

Indian involvement in Afghanistan though comprehensive and well laid, has suffered from a few weaknesses. These shortcomings have been—

1. Firstly, the over reliance that India has had on America especially with regards to handling Pakistan and managing ground security has made India's foreign policy look dis-jointed and cumbersome[57].
2. Secondly Indian assets in Afghanistan especially those from the private sector and NGOs are operating without enough security. As mentioned before, there is a major lack of Indian boots in Afghanistan. India has been reluctant to take greater security measures as it seeks not to antagonise Pakistan[58].
3. Indian establishment has failed to convince western powers engaged in Afghanistan that there are no good or moderate and bad or extremist factions of Taliban and that Taliban as a whole is an insurgent entity that poses grave risk to a stable future in Afghanistan. This has also given an opportunity to Pakistan to take part in such talks and help in wooing the so called moderate factions of Taliban. Potentially, this can lead to a situation where in the pro Pakistan factions of Taliban become power holders in post ISAF Kabul and accordingly restrict Indian mission in the country.
4. Indian establishment has also failed to be assertive enough and position itself as a major stakeholder. While, Indian contribution has been appreciated, Indian concerns and opinions regarding Afghanistan's future have not been given due importance in matters like engaging in talks with the so called moderate factions of the Taliban.
5. India has also been reluctant to gradually diversify its aid from the socio-economic sector to more inclusive business and industry focused action. Its failure to recognise the immense scope of energy security and minerals that the region holds allows other countries especially China to acquire mines with relative ease.
6. India has also suffered a loss of face at the Sharm-al-Shaikh statement fiasco in 2009, since Pakistan's claims of Indian aid to Afghanistan being a smoke screen for anti-Pakistan actions were somewhat validated.

Risks Posed to India's Afghan Mission

Post-ISAF withdrawal, India faces several risks like—

1. There could be a surge in terror attacks on Indian soil and along Indo-Pakistan border especially from major terror groups like Lashkar e Toiba which operate from Afghan territory. With the civilian population back home in frenzy, India will find it difficult to continue with their mission in Afghanistan[59].
2. Indian assets and personnel in Afghanistan could be under severe threat from local militant groups in Afghanistan. In the recent past there have been some devastating attacks on Indian assets in Afghanistan that has led to loss of life and limb. This can demoralise the personnel involved[60].
3. India-Pakistan rivalry could worsen up with the immense trust deficit between the two countries spiralling into a possible full scale armed conflict, especially since Pakistan has viewed Indian involvement as some kind of intrusion into its backyard[61].
4. With change in governments in both India and Afghanistan, there exists a new sense of uncertainty. While Hamid Karzai had warm relations with Indian establishment, Ashraf Ghani brings with him a sense of being unknown. He has also made significant overtures to Pakistan and China, thus relaying a departure from Karzai's diplomatic policies. This can potentially lead to trust deficits cropping up between the two countries. However, things can only become clear post Ghani's Delhi visit slated for April, 2015.

India's Future Course of Action

In the midst of such uncertainties, India faces severe challenges in the near future. With stability still absent in the Afghan society, India has to come up with a comprehensive plan of action for the future and must correct its mistakes of the past. Therefore, the primary questions that comes up are:

1. Should India continue its current levels of commitment in Afghanistan and also provide it with greater military aid?
2. What steps can India take with other regional and global stakeholders in Afghanistan to maintain stability in the war torn state?

   With regards to the first question, Indian involvement in Afghanistan has been vital and widely appreciated by a vast section of Afghan populace and across ethnicities. India and Afghanistan have a long-standing record of technical and economic cooperation in various fields, since prior to 1979 Afghanistan was the largest partner in India's technical and economic cooperation program[62]. Any downscaling now can potentially put an end to all the good work done till now. Indian involvement is also vital to ensure that the country does not fall back in Taliban control again. Thus, Indian civilian aid must continue. However, India must become bolder and try and complement their civilian aid with appropriate military aid wherever possible.

The India-Afghanistan Strategic Partnership Agreement signed in October 2011 allows India to have a greater role in managing Afghan military affairs. Under the agreement, India provides—though to a limited extent—training support and light military equipment to Afghan forces. India should focus on propping up the Afghan air force, which is heavily dependent on international air support. India can help the Afghan air force to operate its current fleet of 50 helicopters. For Afghan forces, the helicopters are an essential tool for operational air support and for resupplying remote military outposts, so New Delhi should particularly focus on training the technical and maintenance staff, on supplying the necessary spare parts and on improving the Afghan aircrew's medical-evacuation capability. In addition to training and support, India can consider providing the Afghan government with military hardware, including attack helicopters, a handful of fighter aircrafts, armoured vehicles, artillery and tactical communication tools[63]. But, it must also be ensured that this is done in consultation with Ashraf Ghani, especially in the light of his overtures to Pakistan and China and his subsequent cancellation of the list of military items that Karzai had requested from India, in the light of Indian non response[64].

With regards to the second question, India must come up with a comprehensive plan of action regarding their Afghan engagement post ISAF withdrawal in 2014. India must recognise the limits of its unilateral action and try and find out potential allies who will be willing to engage with it jointly to develop Afghanistan, especially those who will be affected post ISAF withdrawal. These allies must share Indian concerns and must chalk out a plan to continue rebuilding and stabilising Afghanistan.

These countries can be specifically—Iran, USA, Pakistan, Russia and China. Minus USA, the rest share borders with Afghanistan and can be expected to undergo a strenuous time in case radical forces take over the country. USA has interests in Afghanistan, primarily to ensure that terrorist forces do not find a safe haven in the country again. India can come up with country and bloc specific plans and create conducive conditions for its Afghan missions to continue their operations.

Indo-Iranian Cooperation

India could jointly work with Iran and try and implement these measures in the future[65]—

1. Iran and India could also explore a trilateral trade and transit agreement with Afghanistan. It would not only facilitate movement of goods through the Iran-Afghanistan land route but also make Pakistan's efforts to restrict the movement of Indian goods through Pakistani territory to Afghanistan, irrelevant by acting as a reasonable alternate route.
2. India and Iran should expedite the development of Iran's Chabahar port as also the missing road link from Chabahar to Afghanistan that would facilitate quicker and efficient trade. India has already committed $100 million towards the development of the port, but can consider increasing the extent of investment by inviting private firms and other like minded regional partners.
3. Both Iran and India have an excellent track record of reconstruction aid in Afghanistan, as well as cordial relations and good will among the population. As a conscious effort, India and Iran could, in conjunction with the Afghan government, identify suitable provinces or parts of them in Central, North or West Afghanistan, which could then be taken up by India or Iran or collectively for all round development. International aid, Afghan governmental support and aid from India and Iran could be routed through a consortium which will then undertake development projects and implement it as a model for modern development.

Indian-Iranian relations could also benefit from the thaw in relationship between America and Iran especially in the midst of the recent nuclear deal signed between them[66]. This could bolster and speeden up the construction of Chabahar port which is struggling to gather different sources of investment as of now[67].

Indo-US Cooperation

With regards to the US, two sets of solutions can be applied in this case[68]—

1. The two could significantly increase the Indian presence in Afghanistan and extend the previously minimal Indian military aid. This might include Indian police and army trainers, military advisors, or even Indian troops conducting combat or peacekeeping operations. This could end up negating all the unfounded fears that Pakistan has with regards to Indian involvement and also make Pakistan re-consider their decision of providing aid to insurgent and terrorist groups.
2. The two could avoid an Indian security presence in Afghanistan, which would provoke the most acute fears in Islamabad, and expand India's civilian role in the country, this could be done hand in hand with American civil involvement over there. This approach might be coupled with public and private assurances that the United States will not simply abandon Afghanistan and in spite of the July 2011 deadline announced by the President—the U.S. will not abandon Pakistan, Afghanistan, or the region.

The current Indo-US relations can afford greater space to Afghan issues and should come up with some comprehensive agreement with respect to Afghanistan as ties have improved significantly in the last few years to allow the same. Since both countries seek mutual benefits with respect to a stable Afghanistan, it might not be too problematic for them to come up with a common agreement in the near future. Support from USA is also vital to ensure that Pakistan does not try and impede Indian efforts with acts of violence in the future.

Indo-Pakistan Cooperation

The Indo-Pakistan paradigm can be solved by encouraging joint projects in Afghanistan between the two countries and encouraging greater trade and business linkages between the three countries. If trust deficit between the two countries is dealt with it can lead to a thaw in bilateral relations as well. It can help the countries develop Afghanistan sooner with some kind of joint socio-economic and if agreed mutual military package[69].

However, this cooperation comes with a lot of caveats. Indian and Pakistani governments have a chequered bilateral record. Bilateral issues like Kashmir, involvement of state protected actors in acts of terror and violence, border disputes and any possible armed conflict are problems that loom large on any such possibility working out.

Pakistan has viewed some pro Pakistan factions of Taliban as a part of its anti-India agenda, specifically for carrying out insurgency against the Indian government in Kashmir[70]. This can lead to a major difference of opinion between the two countries in managing Afghanistan in the future, where in India might not want Taliban to be a power holder in Kabul in any way.

Indo-Russia-China Cooperation

Russia, India and other Central Asian countries can also respond to this challenge by jointly working together through forums like the SCO or the Shanghai Cooperation Organisation, which also has Tajikistan as a member and the RIC i.e. Russia India and China group which can also collectively work towards providing security to Afghanistan if that need arises post US withdrawal[71]. But, the success of such a rainbow coalition is highly dependent on how inter group dynamics work out for instance Indo-China or Russia-China relations[72]. This can end up being a successful coalition of up and coming economic and political powers to make up for the efforts of western led forces via a tacit combination of soft and hard power.

Silver Lining-Ghani's India Visit

Ashraf Ghani's India visit, in many ways dispelled fears that Indo-Afghan ties are on a downswing. Ghani to his credit has walked a tight rope and tried to maintain a balance between Pakistani-Chinese interests and Indian aid.

Before his scheduled visit, the two countries signed a number of treaties like a motor trade agreement and a transit trade agreement treaty, both of which need Pakistan's help to work, show casing about how neither of the countries aim to side-line Pakistan and rather seek its full co-operation. Ghani's speech titled "The (re)birth of the Asian Continental Economy: Regional cooperation and Afghanistan's cooperative advantage" also indicated his intent of accelerating Afghanistan's development through pan-Asian co-operation. As a sign of close ties, he will reside in Rashtrapati Bhavan during his visit, a reminder of how important Afghanistan is to India[73].

India was praised extensively by Ashraf Ghani, who recognised how the close historical ties between the two countries had been bolstered by India's "soft-power". He called India, a close ally, as it fulfilled the criteria of being an immediate neighbour, up and coming world power, its extensive aid network and its pre-existing ties with the Islamic world made it indispensible. He also admonished Pakistan for its insecurities. He promised to work towards strengthening diplomatic ties even further, while requesting for greater aid from Indian private sector[74]. In a joint statement, PM Modi indicated about the importance of Afghanistan's security, thus hinting at a possible change in the Indian policy, which hitherto has been reluctant to involve itself deeply in Afghanistan's security affairs[75]. Therefore, Indo-Afghan ties are seemingly healthy for now, though it will be their joint co-operation in the near future that will determine if stability will prevail over geo-politics in the upcoming years.

Conclusion

Afghanistan is undergoing a rough and eventful period of transition. There is a sense of uncertainty as to who holds the cards in the country. There are too many stakeholders involved as well. There is a deep sense of uncertainty involved. If the situation worsens in Afghanistan, neighboring regions and other parts of the globe are bound to suffer immediate and long term repercussions.

After discussing the various aspects of Indo Afghan relationship, I would like to conclude by stating that Indian involvement in Afghanistan has been very productive and has helped war torn nation immensely. India's intentions have been very clear regarding Afghanistan—a stable neighbourhood could help them deal with lesser acts of insurgency fostered violence. Indian involvement in Afghanistan has been well laid and focused. It has received immensely positive reception from different parts of the Afghan society as well as the Afghan government. Its primary aim has been to help the nation stabilise and rebuild so that radical forces do not take over. Indian aid has helped in capacity building of local Afghan assets. Indian intentions have been straight and humble, to say the least. Ashraf Ghani presents a new challenge to Indian diplomacy as he has not interacted with the Indian establishment before. However, his Delhi visit in 2015 has dispelled fears for now that Indo-Afghan ties are disturbed, on the other hand India's current actions can actually elevate its role in stabilising Afghanistan in the next few years.

However, in spite of its best efforts and intentions, Indian involvement has been viewed with great suspicion by Pakistan. Pakistan has needlessly misinterpreted Indian actions and has indulged in actions to harm Indian interests. Pakistan has orchestrated attacks on Indian missions and personnel to scare away Indian citizens involved. Pakistan also, holds a slight advantage over India as it has received immense support from western countries and has good relations with the current Afghani president Ashraf Ghani. Pakistan has also aligned itself with China pretty smartly to hold a position of importance. Pakistan can potentially destabilise Afghanistan again by helping those factions of insurgent and terrorist groups that they find sharing similar interests—like the Haqqani brothers. There is a need to make them realise that Indian involvement is not in any way "anti-Pakistan" and that a destabilised Afghanistan can create numerous headaches for Pakistan as well by causing humanitarian and security problems.

Western countries are trying to leave Afghanistan in a jiffy without understanding the strategic benefits that they are at the risk of squandering to Taliban, if the insurgency re-surfaces in a big way, in case talks do not materialise. Thus, western countries that lead the ISAF, especially the US, must stay put and not entirely abandon the country or the region. It might take some time though before the situation becomes conducive for ISAF forces to leave in entirety. Therefore, these countries must rather prepare for a long stay than a hasty exit.

With the ISAF involvement coming to an end Indian mission in

Afghanistan is bound to undergo a period of difficulty. It must however not do away with all the good work in that country. It has to take some decision about providing greater military aid and help to Afghanistan security establishment if and when requested and also put its point across to Pakistan. It must also be more assertive and independent and not act as a stooge to western interests. Finally, I believe that India must develop an alliance with like minded countries and prepare a long drawn plan for ensuring that eventually Afghanistan is able to atleast regain its status like the pre 1973 era.

END NOTES

1 Ben Smith and Arabella Thorp, "The legal basis for the invasion of Afghanistan", International Affairs and Defence Section, House of Commons Library, 26 February 2010, p. 3, available at www.parliament.uk/briefing-papers/sn05340.pd. Last visited on 10th April, 2015.

2. *Supra* note 1, p. 5.

3. *Supra* note 1, p. 6.

4. Harish V Pant, "India's Afghan policy: Regional and Global Implications, December 2012, Strategic Studies Institute, p. 5, available at http://www.strategicstudiesinstitute.army.mil/pdffiles/pub1141.pdf. Last visited on 10th April, 2015.

5. *Id.,* note 4.

6. "International Contributions to the War Against Terrorism", *Fact Sheet*, May 22, 2002, Office of Public Affairs, Department of Defense, United States of America, p. 5, available at http://www.defense.gov/news/May2002/d20020523cu.pdf. Last visited on 10th April, 2015.

7. *Id.,* note 6.

8. *Id.,* note 7.

9. David J. Gerleman and Jennifer E. Stevens, "Operation Enduring Freedom: Foreign Pledges of Military & Intelligence Support", Research Associates Foreign Affairs, Defense, and Trade Division and Steven A. Hildreth Specialist in National Defense, Foreign Affairs, Defense, and Trade Division, updated October 17, 2001, CRS Report for Congress, CRS-5, available at http://fpc.state.gov/documents/organization/6207.pdf. Last visited on 10th April, 2015.

10. *Id.,* note 9.

11. Ajay Anil Cherian, "Rebuilding Afghanistan: The role of its neighbours", *International Policy Digest,* 10th December, 2014, available at http://www.internationalpolicydigest.org/2014/10/12/rebuilding-afghanistan-the-role-of-the-its-neighbors/ Last visited on 21st April, 2015.

12. "Hamid Karzai biography", *biography.com*, available at http://www.biography.com/people/hamid-karzai-537356. Last visited on 10th April, 2015.

13. Larry Hanauer and Peter Chalk, "India's and Pakistan's Strategies in Afghanistan-Implications for the United States and the Region", 2012, RAND Centre For Asia-Pacific Policy, International Programmes at RAND, pp. 21 and 22, available at http://www.rand.org/content/dam/rand/pubs/occasional_papers/2012/RAND_OP387.pdf. Last visited on 10th April, 2015.

14. "India and Afghanistan—A Development Partnership", *mea.gov.in*, p. 8, available at http://mea.gov.in/Uploads/PublicationDocs/176_india-and-afghanistan-a-development-partnership.pdf. Last visited on 10th April, 2015.
15. *Supra* note 14, p. 7.
16. "India's growing stake in Afghanistan", *BBC News*, 28 June 2012, available at http://www.bbc.com/news/world-asia-18622573. Last visited on 20th April, 2015.
17. *Supra* note 14, p. 9.
18. *Supra* note 14, p. 10.
19. *Supra* note 14, p. 11.
20. "Indian equipment for Afghan army", *Hindustan Times*, December 23, 2006, available at http://www.hindustantimes.com/nm21/indian-equipment-for-afghan-army/article1-195421.aspx. Last visited on 10th April, 2015.
21. Arvind Gupta, "Strategic partnership with Afghanistan: India showcases it soft power", IDSA comment, October 10, 2011, available at http://www.idsa.in/idsacomments/StrategicPartnershipwithAfghanistanIndiaShowcasesitsSoftPower_agupta_101011. Last visited on 10th April, 2015.
22. *Supra* note 20.
23. Rajeev Sharma, "India-Russia-Afghanistan synergy: India to pay for Russian arms supplies to Kabul", *Russia Today*, available at http://rt.com/op-edge/154288-afghanistan-india-taliban-russia-arms/. Last visited on 10th April, 2015.
24. Atul Chandra, "HAL readies Cheetal delivery for Afghanistan Air Force", *Flightglobal.com*, August 27, 2014, available at http://www.flightglobal.com/news/articles/hal-readies-cheetal-delivery-for-afghanistan-air-force-403076/. Last visited on 10th April, 2015.
25. *Supra* note 4, p. 7.
26. *Supra* note 13, p. 23.
27. "In Afghanistan Indians are praised simply for being Indian", October 9, 2009, Q&A: Jayant Prasad Indian ambassador to Afghanistan, Jyoti Malhotra, available at http://www.business-standard.com/article/economy-policy/-in-afghanistan-indians-are-praised-simply-for-being-indian-109100900012_1.html. Last visited on 10th April, 2015.
28. Harish V. Pant, "India's changing role in the Afghan conflict", Spring 2011, Middle East Quarterly, pp. 31-39, available at http://www.meforum.org/2895/india-afghanistan. Last visited on 13th April, 2015.
29. Jack Healy and Alicia Reuben, "Afghanistan Favors India and denigrates Pakistan", *The New York Times*, 4th October, 2011, available at http://www.nytimes.com/2011/10/05/world/asia/afghanistan-curries-favor-with-india-and-denigrates-pakistan.html?_r=1. Last visited on 13th April, 2015.
30. *Supra* note 21.
31. Tahir Khan, "Afghanistan calls India an all weather friend", *The Express Tribune with the International New York Times*, October 22, 2014, available at http://www.worldaffairsjournal.org/content/afghanistan-calls-india-all-weather-friend. Last visited on 10th April, 2015.
32. Nupur Basu, "Guns and roses in Kabul", *The Hindu*, 11th October, 2011, available at http://www.thehindu.com/todays-paper/tp-opinion/guns-and-roses-in-kabul/article2557147.ece. Last visited on 13th April, 2015.
33. Rajiv Agarwal, "Post 2014 Afghanistan: Policy options for India and Iran", Institute of Peace and Conflict Studies, available at http://www.ipcs.org/issue-brief/iran/post-2014-afghanistan-policy-options-for-india-and-iran-247.html. Last visited on 10th April, 2015
34. Zia Sarhadi, "Ashraf Ghani: An Afghan in a hurry", Crescent International, December,

2014, available at http://www.crescent-online.net/2014/12/ashraf-ghani-an-aghan-in-a-hurry-zia-sarhadi-4748-articles.html. Last visited on 13th April, 2015.

35. Gareth Price, "India's policy towards Afghanistan", August 2013, Chatham House, p. 3, available at http://www.chathamhouse.org/sites/files/chathamhouse/public/Research/Asia/0813pp_indiaafghanistan.pdf. Last visited on 10th April, 2015.
36. Alistair Scrutton and Arup Roy Chowdhry, "In India Karzai reaches out to brother Pakistan", *Reuters News Agency*, 5th October, 2011, available at http://www.reuters.com/article/2011/10/05/us-afghanistan-india-idUSTRE79417D20111005. Last visited on 13th April, 2015.
37. "NATO strikes transport deals to bypass Afghanistan", *CBS news*, 4th June, 2012, available at http://www.cbsnews.com/news/nato-strikes-transport-deals-to-bypass-pakistan/. Last visited on 13th April, 2015.
38. Phil Gasper, "Afghanistan, the CIA, Bin Laden and the Taliban", Third World Traveller, *International Socialist Review*, November-December, 2001, available at http://www.thirdworldtraveler.com/Afghanistan/Afghanistan_CIA_Taliban.html. Last visited on 13th April, 2015.
39. Richard Fontaine, "U.S.-India Strategic Dialogue"—Moving Ahead in Afghanistan: The U.S.-India-Pakistan Dynamic, CII-Aspen strategy group, pp.2 and 3, available at http://www.aspeninstitute.org/sites/default/files/content/upload/ASG_Fontaine_Moving_Ahead_Afghanistan.pdf, last visited 10th April, 2015.
40. *Id.,* note 39.
41. "India, Afghanistan nexus and Pakistan", *Dawn* Newspaper, 24th May, 2013, available at http://www.dawn.com/news/1027538/afghanistan-india-nexus-pakistan. Last visited on 15th June, 2015.
42. Munir Akram, "India's great power game", *Dawn* newspaper, 28th May, 2014, available at http://www.dawn.com/news/1134772. Last visited on 15th June, 2015.
43. Musa Khan Jalalzai, "India and the future of Afghanistan", *Daily Times*, October 29, 2014, available at http://www.dailytimes.com.pk/opinion/29-Oct-2014/india-and-the-future-of-afghanistan. Last visited on 20th June 2015.
44. *Supra* note 13, p. 7.
45. *Supra* note 14.
46. *Id.,* note 45.
47. *Id.,* note 46.
48. "Terror safe havens within Pak unacceptable: Obama", November 8, 2010, available at http://www.rediff.com/news/report/slide-show-1-obama-visit-what-obama-said-about-pakistan-un-and-afghanistan/20101108.htm. Last visited on 10th April, 2015.
49. *Supra* note 4, p. 12.
50. *Supra* note 4, pp. 12-13.
51. *Supra* note 4, p. 14.
52. *Supra* note 4, p. 3.
53. *Supra* note 13, pp. 7-8.
54. *Supra* note 4, p. 12.
55. *Supra* note 48.
56. "US slaps sanctions on Taliban's Haqqani network", *ndtv.com*, July 23, 2010, available at http://www.ndtv.com/world-news/us-slaps-sanctions-on-talibans-haqqani-network-424768. Last visited on 20th April, 2015.
57. *Supra* note 4, p. 11.
58. *Supra* note 4, p. 13.

59. "Assessing India's position on NATO's Afghanistan pullout", 24th November, 2014, available at http://www.dw.de/assessing-indias-position-on-natos-afghanistan-pullout/a-18082481. Last visited on 13th April, 2015.
60. *Id.,* note 59.
61. *Id.,* note 60.
62. *Supra* note 4, p. 8.
63. Javid Ahmad, "Should India provide direct military aid to Afghanistan?", *The New York Times*, May 14, 2013, available at http://india.blogs.nytimes.com/2013/05/14/should-india-provide-direct-military-aid-to-afghanistan/?_r=1, Last visited on 10th April, 2015.
64. Praveen Swami, "Upset with delay, Kabul shelves arms request from Delhi", *The Indian Express*, October 30, 2014, available at http://indianexpress.com/article/india/india-others/upset-with-delay-kabul-shelves-request-for-arms-aid-from-delhi/. Last visited on 22nd April, 2015.
65. *Supra* note 33.
66. "As it happened: Iran nuclear deal", *bbc.com*, available at http://www.bbc.com/news/world-middle-east-25075776. Last visited on 13th April, 2015.
67. Wendy Laursen, "Modi marks out his territory", *The Maritime Executive*, 15th March, 2015, available at http://www.maritime-executive.com/article/modi-marks-out-his-territory. Last visited on 13th April, 2015.
68. *Supra* note 39, pp. 3 and 4.
69. *Supra* note 38, p. 5.
70. Ashraf Wani, "Pakistan army fooled youth for blood game in Kashmir says Tehreek e Taliban, Pakistan", *India Today*, December 28, 2014, available at http://indiatoday.intoday.in/story/pakistan-army-tehreek-e-taliban-pakistan-pak-army-fooled-youth-for-blood-game-in-kashmir-says-ttp/1/409279.html. Last visited on 23rd April, 2015.
71. Dmitri Trenin, Oleg Kulakov, Alexey Malashenko and Petr Topychkanov, "A Russian Strategy for Afghanistan After the Coalition Troop Withdrawal", May 22, 2014, Carnegie Moscow Center, available at http://carnegie.ru/publications/?fa=55669#. Last visited on 13th April, 2015.
72. Abanti Bhattacharya, "The fallacy in the India-China-Russia Triangle", Vol. 28, Issue 2, Commentaries, April 2004, IDSA Journal, available at http://www.idsa.in/strategicanalysis/TheFallacyintheRussiaIndiaChinaTriangle_abhattacharya_0404.html. Last visited on 13th April, 2015.
73. Suhasini Haider, "Slew of pacts under discussion ahead of Ghani visit", April 23, 2015, *The Hindu*, available at http://www.thehindu.com/news/national/slew-of-pacts-under-discussion-ahead-of-ghani-visit/article7131002.ece. Last visited on 20th June, 2015.
74. John Cherian, "Recharging relations", *Frontline*, May 29, 2015.
75. Farid Hussain Khail, "President Ghani meets his Indian counterpart", *Tolo news*, 29th April, 2015, available at http://www.tolonews.com/en/afghanistan/19289-president-ghani-meets-his-indian-counterpart . Last visited on 25th June, 2015.

Index